The Heart of Christmas

Sarah Bubbers read English at the University College of Wales, Aberystwyth, before joining the editorial staff of a London publisher. She worked on children's books, religious books and fiction before becoming a freelance editor. She is married with twin baby sons who were born during work on this book, and whose first word may well be "Christmas".

THE
HEART OF
CHRISTMAS

Compiled by Sarah Bubbers

Foreword by HRH Princess Alexandra
Royalties in aid of Crisis at Christmas

Collins
FOUNT PAPERBACKS

First published in Great Britain
by Fount Paperbacks, London in 1987
Second impression December 1987

Copyright in the original items
and text, unless otherwise stated,
© William Collins Sons & Co Ltd, 1987

Copyright in the editorial arrangement
© Sarah Bubbers 1987

Printed and bound in Great Britain by
William Collins Sons & Co. Ltd, Glasgow

The Acknowledgements on pages 139–41
are an extension of this copyright page

Contents

Foreword by HRH Princess Alexandra   7

1 **Away in a Manger**   11
A Child's Christmas

2 **Love Came Down at Christmas**   45
God's Wonderful Gift

3 **O Come, All Ye Faithful**   75
Christmas Remembered

4 **See Amid the Winter's Snow**   103
The Challenge of Christmas

In Case You Didn't Know . . .   133

Acknowledgements   139

Foreword

I am delighted to be associated with Crisis at Christmas and, as Patron, wholeheartedly support the marvellous work of helping the homeless.

Many people perhaps know of the charity's annual "Open Christmas", when hundreds of volunteers help to provide food, warmth, clothing, medical attention and companionship for those who have nowhere else to go during the holiday. Fewer, however, are probably aware of the other vital, ongoing work of fund-raising throughout the year for projects that support the single homeless and increase awareness of their problems.

Most of us will have warm homes and families to enjoy this Christmas but, because many are not so fortunate, I commend this book to you. It serves as a reminder to us all of the dedicated work being carried out by Crisis at Christmas for those who need our help and, surely, it conveys anew the wonder of the Christmas story – the child who was born in a manger, yet who was the Saviour of the world.

1987

Alexandra

The Editor would like to thank all those extremely busy people who have written items especially for this book, and the authors and publishers who have given their works free of charge.

1
Away in a Manger
A Child's Christmas

✠

In the sixth month of Elizabeth's pregnancy God sent the angel Gabriel to a town in Galilee named Nazareth. He had a message for a girl promised in marriage to a man named Joseph, who was a descendant of King David. The girl's name was Mary. The angel came to her and said, "Peace be with you! The Lord is with you and has greatly blessed you!"

Mary was deeply troubled by the angel's message, and she wondered what his words meant. The angel said to her, "Don't be afraid, Mary; God has been gracious to you. You will become pregnant and give birth to a son, and you will name him Jesus. He will be great and will be called the Son of the Most High God. The Lord God will make him a king, as his ancestor David was, and he will be the king of the descendants of Jacob for ever; his kingdom will never end!"

Mary said to the angel, "I am a virgin. How, then, can this be?"

The angel answered, "The Holy Spirit will come on you, and God's power will rest upon you. For this reason the holy child will be called the Son of God. Remember your relative Elizabeth. It is said that she cannot have children, but she herself is now six months pregnant, even though she is very old. For there is nothing that God cannot do."

"I am the Lord's servant," said Mary; "may it happen to me as you have said." And the angel left her.

(Luke 1:26–38)

✠

Alvin Stardust

When I think of Christmas the first thing that comes to mind is the carol "Away in a Manger". I think this is because it was the very first song I ever learnt as a small child, and the same is probably true for most children. I can remember being taught it when I started school. Now I have children of my own and they sing it too.

Away in a manger, no crib for a bed,
The little Lord Jesus laid down his sweet head.
The stars in the bright sky looked down where he lay,
The little Lord Jesus asleep on the hay.

The cattle are lowing, the baby awakes,
But little Lord Jesus, no crying he makes.
I love thee, Lord Jesus! Look down from the sky,
And stay by my side until morning is nigh.

Be near me, Lord Jesus; I ask thee to stay
Close by me for ever, and love me, I pray.
Bless all the dear children in thy tender care,
And fit us for heaven, to live with thee there.

David Kossoff

The Three Donkeys was written as "a first try at a New Testament story" after the tremendous success of David Kossoff's radio and television stories from the Old Testament.

When I tell people, as I now tell you, that now comes a story about three donkeys in heaven, it has some odd effects. One of the oddest is that many people who have always said they don't believe in heaven are rather offended at the thought that donkeys should be allowed in. Very illogical. If heaven is for people who are rather nice, why not for donkeys, who in the main are nicer than people? Most animals are, don't you agree?

Anyway, three donkeys, spending an afternoon together in heaven. They'd all been there a long time. Centuries. By accident they'd discovered that they'd all come from the same part of the world, and had arrived in heaven, give or take a few years, at the same time. Very pleasant and interesting for them. They all looked rather alike. Well, donkeys do. They were lying in the shade. One of them was telling his story, and the other two were very interested. Are you?

The First Donkey

The first donkey said, "I had a number of masters, but I remember one better than I do the others. Not because of *him* so much – although he was a very kind and gentle man – but more because of one or two strange things that happened during the time I worked for him. He was a carpenter, and he worked and lived in Nazareth. Not a rich man. Not many possessions. I don't think he would have bought me but there'd been a Roman order that made it necessary for him to go to Bethlehem. A census was being taken. Anyway, he bought me so that my mistress could ride there. You see, she was going to have a baby – and pretty soon too. And she had to go to Bethlehem as well; it was a Roman order and nobody ever argued with a Roman order. So we went. Took a long time. I trod as soft as I could.

"When we got there it was late at night and the town was bursting with people. The inns and rooming houses were packed. No room anywhere. The last innkeeper my master asked at least *tried* to help. He said his stable was dry and warm and we could spend the night there. I was a bit worried for my mistress, in her condition. I mean, I've slept in stables all my life but she was a rather refined, well-brought-up, quiet sort of person. My master settled her down as comfortably as he could. He loaded the largest manger with hay and straw from all the others and she lay on that.

"Well, I must have dozed off. The thing that woke me up was the sound of men's voices. At first I thought it was the Romans but then I saw it was a crowd of shepherds. They were excited. Some were praying. On the manger lay my mistress and in her arms her newborn baby. As far as I could make out, these shepherds in the middle of the night had been told by a whole *army* of angels that my mistress's baby was something very special. They were told where to come and see for themselves, and then to go and spread the word that this baby, born in a stable shared by me and two other donkeys and a cow, was going to change the world!

"Well, people *did* get excited, but not for long. Mind you, one good thing – one or two people helped my master find somewhere to live in Bethlehem till my mistress felt stronger. They lived very quietly. No miracles. You'd have thought that exciting night had never happened. I'd nearly forgotten it. Well, about six months after that night we had another big night. Not shepherds this time. No, not shepherds – more like princes! There were three of them, all from different places far away. Servants by the dozen, camels, a fine old to-do. They blocked the street! They also spoke of angels, and a great star in the sky, which had guided them, and special signs which, because they were all three of them very wise men, they knew had meant that our baby was special.

" 'A saviour', they said. 'A king', they said. 'Greater by far than King Herod', they said. Well, when I heard that I knew there'd be trouble. I was right. The next morning the wise men had gone. And by midday so were we. Seems God had told my master to take the special baby and the special baby's mother and the special baby's donkey and get far away *fast* because King Herod was cross. We went down to Egypt, I remember."

The first donkey looked at the other two. "There must have been something *very* special about our baby," he said, "though I must say in the six years I was with the family *I* never noticed anything."

Little Donkey

Little donkey, little donkey,
on a dusty road,
got to keep on plodding onward
with your precious load:

Been a long time, little donkey,
through the winter's night –
don't give up now, little donkey,
Bethlehem's in sight.
  Ring out those bells tonight,
  Bethlehem, Bethlehem;
  follow that star tonight,
  Bethlehem, Bethlehem!

17

Little donkey, little donkey,
had a heavy day –
little donkey, carry Mary
safely on her way.
    Little donkey, carry Mary
    safely on her way.

Eric Boswell

Jesus, Our Brother, Kind and Good

Jesus, our brother, kind and good,
Was humbly born in a stable rude;
And the friendly beasts around him stood,
Jesus, our brother, kind and good.

"I," said the donkey, shaggy and brown,
"I carried his mother uphill and down,
I carried her safely to Bethlehem town.
I," said the donkey, shaggy and brown.

"I," said the cow, all white and red,
"I gave him my manger for a bed,
I gave him my hay to pillow his head.
I," said the cow, all white and red.

"I," said the sheep with the curly horn,
"I gave him my wool for a blanket warm.
He wore my coat on Christmas morn.
I," said the sheep with the curly horn.

"I," said the dove from the rafters high,
"I cooed him to sleep so he would not cry,
We cooed him to sleep, my mate and I.
I," said the dove from the rafters high.

Robin's Red Breast

JEAN CHAPMAN

A big black bird, the raven, had stayed out far too long. It was dark when he came flying back to his roost. The wind buffeted and pushed him about, forcing him to beat his wings strongly as he flew over the houses of Bethlehem.

He had hardly left the town behind him when suddenly the sky filled with light. It seemed brighter than starlight, brighter than moonlight. Below him the raven could clearly see sheep on a hillside, and a cornfield. He saw shepherds standing near a fire, staring upward into the sky behind the raven.

The bird swerved, turning about to look back at Bethlehem and the light. It was made by a star brighter than a thousand lanterns.

"The Christ Child has been born!" croaked the raven. "I must tell the other birds at once." He soared away, high in the air, flying fast to wake the wren.

"Wake up! Wake up, Wren!" shouted the raven. "Wake up! The Child is born. His star shines *now* in the sky!"

"I am awake. I can hear you", called the wren. "I will go to see the Baby at once. I'll take him a blanket, softly woven from leaves and moss."

"And I will go and wake the cock", flustered the raven.

"Rooster! Rooster! Wake your hens!" shouted the raven. "The Child is born. I have seen his star."

Chu-chu-choooook! The rooster flapped and fussed. *Ch*-chu-chooooook! His hens were already awake, clucking and crooning about him. "I must tell the world that the Babe is born", the rooster told them. *Pffft!* He puffed out his chest. "I shall say, *cock-a-doodle-doo! Cock-a-doo! No!* No, I will not. Cock-a-doodle does not sound important enough."

"What shall you say then?" clucked the hens.

"I shall crow. I shall crow in my most beautiful tones", said the rooster. "And I only have until dawn to practise. Listen now, hens, how is this?" And the rooster doodled and doodled and doodled.

At dawn he stood on a fence and his crowing was heard all over Bethlehem. "*Christus natus est!*" he shouted joyfully in the old language of Latin. It sounded important. His hens were proud and his hens were surprised. None of them had heard the rooster crow in anything but doodles before.

By then the raven had found the nightingale. Her voice was far sweeter than the rooster's, sweeter than any other bird's. She flew to the stable to sing to the Christ Child.

Other birds came flying to the stable. They came from trees, from the tall grass, from bushes and shrubs. Among them was a little brown robin, too small to be noticed and heartsick as he listened to the nightingale's song. He too had hoped to chirp his good-morning greeting to the Baby, but it would be dull music to hear after the nightingale's glorious song. He wished there was a way to show his joy and to give the Child a gift, but the robin could not fly strongly like the raven. He could not weave like the wren. He could not crow like the cock. He could not sing like the nightingale.

The robin hopped a little closer to the stable door. He saw the manger-bed was close to the fire. And he saw a flame suddenly leap higher than the rest. Would its heat redden the Baby's cheeks?

Swiftly the robin flew through the door, into the stable. With widely spread wings he fluttered between the fire and the Child's head. He hovered there, hardly moving. Faster and faster and faster beat his wings until they whirred like a fan. He stayed there until Mary lifted the Baby from his bed. By then, the robin's breast-feathers were scorched by the fire's heat.

And since that morning, every robin's breast is the colour of a bright flame. It may be scarlet-red, or orange, or yellow. Look for a robin and see for yourself.

A Christmas Story

RACHEL BILLINGTON

Once upon a time there were three children called Edward, Charlotte and Laura. They were brothers and sisters.

Edward was ten and very tall and strong; he rode a huge bicycle. Charlotte was eight and knew all her tables and could stand on her head. Laura was not yet five and couldn't do very much at all except play with her dolls.

They lived with their mother and father in a small house deep in the Dorset countryside. Although the house was small, the garden was big and filled with flowers and shrubs and even some little trees.

Laura loved to wander out there and play on the lawn. When Edward and Charlotte were busy, which was rather often, she set up her dolls on the steps and pretended they were her family. If the sun was hot, she took them under a little tree whose branches drooped down like an umbrella. If it was wet, she went there even quicker.

It was a very special tree. In autumn it had bright red balls growing off it. Laura's mother told her they were crab-apples. Her mother had forbidden her to eat them because they were so sour. She never picked them either, so they stayed on the tree long after the other fruit had gone. Even when the leaves turned from green to gold to brown and then fell right off. Sometimes Laura felt sorry for them hanging alone out there in the cold and dark.

One winter afternoon Laura, dressed in gumboots and thick coat, was walking in the garden. It was late and the sun had just set, casting a red glow all around. It looked very beautiful. But Laura was sad.

Tonight was Christmas Eve. Usually she was very happy, looking forward to the celebrations. But this year a terrible

21

thing had happened. She had no present for her mother, not even a card.

Edward had saved up his pocket money and bought a gold pen. Charlotte had sewed a little velvet needle case at school. But Laura, who had only a few pence when her father remembered, and didn't go to school, had nothing. She had made a card some time ago, but it got lost and anyway it wasn't very good. So Laura, who loved her mother very much and wanted to give her the best present in the world, felt very sad. She walked slowly up the path, scuffing her gumboots.

Her mother had said the Christmas tree looked very dull this year. "It won't be like Christmas with such a dull-looking tree", she had said.

If only she was clever enough to make a star or a fairy doll. She looked up across the lawn, and suddenly she had the most wonderful idea. Her face broke into a wide smile and she began to run.

She had not gone far before there was a cry from the house. "Laura! Laura! Where are you?" It was her mother. Laura stopped.

"Laura, what are you doing out there? It's almost dark. Come in now and help me hang up your stocking."

So Laura went inside. But she didn't give up her idea. The next morning, after the excitement of opening their stockings was over but before breakfast when they gave each other presents, she crept downstairs to the back door. She pulled it open. Then she gasped with surprise for the green garden had turned white. It had snowed overnight.

The brightness and ice-cold air made her eyes water. Even so she didn't hesitate. With a little basket over her arm, she stepped outside.

Her heart beat fast in a frightened way, for the garden seemed bigger than usual and it was difficult to walk in the snow. Her hands were soon so red and cold that she could hardly feel them.

At length she reached the place where the little tree stood. But, to her dismay, the branches were completely bare, jutting out like dark fingers. Where were the apples?

She looked round carefully and suddenly noticed little snowy lumps under the tree. She bent down and began to dig in the icy whiteness.

Laura's mother had laid out breakfast in the warm and cheerful kitchen. "Oh!" she exclaimed at the pile of presents at her place. "How lovely!" Then she looked round. "Where's Laura?"

At that moment, the door opened and in walked Laura. Everybody peered round. There was snow in her hair and she looked almost frozen with cold. She walked quickly up to her mother and brought from behind her back the little basket. There lay the reddest, shiniest, most beautiful little round apples you'd ever seen.

"They're for the Christmas tree, Mummy!" said Laura.

"Oh, darling!" cried her mother. "Have you been out in all that snow for me?"

Laura only smiled.

And Laura's mother was so pleased that she took the apples straight away and tied a little twist of silk round each stalk and hung them on the tree.

The whole family stood back admiringly. They bobbed so prettily, so bright, so cheerful.

"Now you can have a happy Christmas, Mummy", said Laura. "And they can too."

Snowflakes

And did you know
That every flake of snow
That forms so high
In the grey winter sky
And falls so far,
Is a bright six-pointed star?
Each crystal grows
A flower as perfect as a rose.
Lace could never make
The patterns of a flake.
No brooch
Of figured silver could approach
Its delicate craftsmanship. And think:
Each pattern is distinct.
Of all the snowflakes floating there –
The million million in the air –
None is the same. Each star
Is newly forged, as faces are,
Shaped to its own design
Like yours and mine.
And yet . . . each one
Melts when its flight is done;
Holds frozen loveliness
A moment, even less;
Suspends itself in time —
And passes like a rhyme.

Clive Sansom

Christmas at Mole End
from *The Wind in the Willows*

KENNETH GRAHAME

The Mole never dreams of the adventures that lie ahead when he leaves his spring cleaning and finds his way to the river. For there he meets the Rat, who introduces him to all sorts of new experiences and new friends, including Toad and Badger. As Christmas approaches, Mole longs to go home. Yet his arrival at Mole End is bleak, for the house is cold and dark and there isn't even any food to offer the Rat, who is soon given a guided tour of his friend's home . . .

At last the Rat succeeded in decoying him to the table, and had just got seriously to work with the sardine-opener when sounds were heard from the fore-court without – sounds like a scuffling of small feet in the gravel and a confused murmur of tiny voices, while broken sentences reached them – "Now, all in a line – hold the lantern up a bit, Tommy – clear your throats first – no coughing after I say one, two, three. – Where's young Bill? – Here, come on, do, we're all a-waiting –"

"What's up?" inquired the Rat, pausing in his labours.

"I think it must be the field-mice", replied the Mole, with a touch of pride in his manner. "They go round carol-singing regularly at this time of the year. They're quite an institution in these parts. And they never pass me over – they come to Mole End last of all; and I used to give them hot drinks, and supper too sometimes, when I could afford it. It will be like old times to hear them again."

"Let's have a look at them!" cried the Rat, jumping up and running to the door.

It was a pretty sight, and a seasonable one, that met their eyes when they flung the door open. In the forecourt, lit by the dim rays of a horn lantern, some eight or ten little field-mice stood in a semicircle, red worsted comforters round their throats, their fore-paws thrust deep into their pockets, their feet jigging for warmth. With bright beady eyes they glanced shyly at each other, sniggering a little, sniffing and applying coat-sleeves a good deal. As the door opened, one of the elder ones that carried the lantern was just saying, "Now then, one, two, three!" and forthwith their shrill little voices uprose on the air, singing one of the old-time carols that their fore-fathers composed in fields that were fallow and held by frost, or when snow-bound in chimney corners, and handed down to be sung in the miry street to lamp-lit windows at Yule-time.

Carol

Villagers all, this frosty tide,
Let your doors swing open wide,
Though wind may follow, and snow beside,
Yet draw us in by your fire to bide;
  Joy shall be yours in the morning!

Here we stand in the cold and the sleet,
Blowing fingers and stamping feet,
Come from far away you to greet —
You by the fire and we in the street —
  Bidding you joy in the morning!

For ere one half of the night was gone,
Sudden a star has led us on,
Raining bliss and benison —
Bliss tomorrow and more anon,
  Joy for every morning!

Goodman Joseph toiled through the snow –
Saw the star o'er a stable low;
Mary she might not further go –
Welcome thatch, and litter below!
  Joy was hers in the morning!

And then they heard the angels tell
"Who were the first to cry Nowell?
Animals all, as it befell,
In the stable where they did dwell!
  Joy shall be theirs in the morning!"

The voices ceased, the singers, bashful but smiling, exchanged sidelong glances, and silence succeeded – but for a moment only. Then, from up above and far away, down the tunnel they had so lately travelled, was borne to their ears in a faint musical hum the sound of distant bells ringing a joyful and clangorous peal.

"Very well sung, boys!" cried the Rat heartily. "And now come along in, all of you, and warm yourselves by the fire, and have something hot!"

"Yes, come along, field-mice", cried the Mole eagerly. "This is quite like old times! Shut the door after you. Pull up that settle to the fire. Now, you just wait a minute, while we – O, Ratty!" he cried in despair, plumping down on a seat, with tears impending. "Whatever are we doing? We've nothing to give them!"

"You leave all that to me", said the masterful Rat. "Here, you with the lantern! Come over this way. I want to talk to you. Now, tell me, are there any shops open at this hour of the night?"

"Why, certainly, sir", replied the field-mouse respectfully. "At this time of the year our shops keep open to all sorts of hours."

"Then look here!" said the Rat. "You go off at once, you and your lantern, and you get me –"

Here much muttered conversation ensued, and the Mole only heard bits of it, such as – "Fresh, mind! – no, a pound of that will do – see you get Buggins's, for I won't have any other – no, only the best – if you can't get it there, try somewhere else – yes, of course, home-made, no tinned stuff – well then, do the best you can!" Finally, there was a chink of coin passing from paw to paw, the field-mouse was provided with an ample basket for his purchases, and off he hurried, he and his lantern.

The rest of the field-mice, perched in a row on the settle, their small legs swinging, gave themselves up to the enjoyment of the fire, and toasted their chilblains till they tingled; while the Mole, failing to draw them into easy conversation, plunged into family history and made each of them recite the names of their numerous brothers, who were too young, it appeared, to be allowed to go out a-carolling this year, but looked forward very shortly to winning the parental consent.

The Rat, meanwhile, was busy examining the label on one of the beer-bottles. "I perceive this to be Old Burton", he remarked approvingly. "*Sensible* Mole! The very thing! Now we shall be able to mull some ale! Get the things ready, Mole, while I draw the corks."

It did not take long to prepare the brew and thrust the tin heater well into the red heart of the fire; and soon every field-mouse was sipping and coughing and choking (for a little mulled ale goes a long way) and wiping his eyes and laughing and forgetting he had ever been cold in all his life.

"They act plays too, these fellows", the Mole explained to the Rat. "Make them up all by themselves, and act them afterwards. And very well they do it, too! They gave us a capital one last year, about a field-mouse who was captured at sea by a Barbary corsair, and made to row in a galley; and when he escaped and got home again, his lady-love had gone into a convent. Here, *you*! You were in it, I remember. Get up and recite a bit."

The field-mouse addressed got up on his legs, giggled

shyly, looked round the room, and remained absolutely tongue-tied. His comrades cheered him on, Mole coaxed and encouraged him, and the Rat went so far as to take him by the shoulders and shake him; but nothing could overcome his stage-fright. They were all busily engaged on him like watermen applying the Royal Humane Society's regulations to a case of long submersion, when the latch clicked, the door opened, and the field-mouse with the lantern reappeared, staggering under the weight of his basket.

There was no more talk of play-acting once the very real and solid contents of the basket had been tumbled out on the table. Under the generalship of Rat, everybody was set to do something or to fetch something. In a very few minutes supper was ready, and Mole, as he took the head of the table in a sort of dream, saw a lately barren board set thick with savoury comforts; saw his little friends' faces brighten and beam as they fell to without delay; and then let himself loose – for he was famished indeed – on the provender so magically provided, thinking what a happy home-coming this had turned out, after all.

Holly

Its head it points to heaven
And shows its berries red
In token of the drops of blood
Which on Calvary were shed

And in the holly prickles
You can plainly see
The crown of thorns our Saviour wore
When going up to Calvary.

And although up in heaven
His love can still be seen
In the holly colour,
The everlasting green.

Christmas arrives in Narnia
from *The Lion, the Witch and the Wardrobe*

C.S. LEWIS

When Lucy, Susan, Peter and Edmund enter the Professor's mysterious wardrobe, they find themselves in the enchanted world of Narnia. The land is in the power of the evil White Witch, who ordains that it will always be winter yet never Christmas. But now it is said that Aslan, the Lion King, is back to free the country and bring springtime. The children, with their friends the Beavers, set out in a desperate bid to reach Aslan, but on their way they meet someone very familiar . . .

. . . It seemed to Lucy only the next minute (though really it was hours and hours later) when she woke up feeling a little cold and dreadfully stiff, and thinking how she would like a hot bath. Then she felt a set of long whiskers tickling her cheek and saw the cold daylight coming in through the mouth of the cave. But immediately after that she was very wide awake indeed, and so was everyone else. In fact they were all sitting up with their mouths and eyes wide open, listening to a sound which was the very sound they'd all been thinking of (and sometimes imagining they heard) during their walk last night. It was a sound of jingling bells.

Mr Beaver was out of the cave like a flash the moment he heard it. Perhaps you think, as Lucy thought for a moment, that this was a very silly thing to do? But it was really a very sensible one. He knew he could scramble to the top of the bank among bushes and brambles without being seen; and he wanted above all things to see which way the Witch's sledge went. The others all sat in the cave waiting and wondering.

They waited nearly five minutes. Then they heard something that frightened them very much. They heard voices. "Oh," thought Lucy, "he's been seen. She's caught him!" Great was their surprise when, a little later, they heard Mr Beaver's voice calling to them from just outside the cave.

"It's all right", he was shouting. "Come out, Mrs Beaver. Come out, Sons and Daughters of Adam. It's all right! It isn't *Her*!" This was bad grammar of course, but that is how beavers talk when they are excited; I mean, in Narnia – in our world they usually don't talk at all.

So Mrs Beaver and the children came bundling out of the cave, all blinking in the daylight, and with earth all over them, and looking very frowsty and unbrushed and uncombed and with the sleep in their eyes.

"Come on!" cried Mr Beaver, who was almost dancing with delight. "Come and see! This is a nasty knock for the Witch! It looks as if her power was already crumbling."

"What *do* you mean, Mr Beaver?" panted Peter as they all scrambled up the steep bank of the valley together.

"Didn't I tell you," answered Mr Beaver, "that she'd made it always winter and never Christmas? Didn't I tell you? Well, just come and see!"

And then they were all at the top and did see.

It *was* a sledge, and it *was* reindeer with bells on their harness. But they were far bigger than the Witch's reindeer, and they were not white but brown. And on the sledge sat a person whom everyone knew the moment they set eyes on him. He was a huge man in a bright red robe (bright as holly berries) with a hood that had fur inside it and a great white beard that fell like a foamy waterfall over his chest. Everyone knew him because, though you see people of his sort only in Narnia, you see pictures of them and hear them talked about even in our world – the world on this side of the wardrobe door. But when you really see them in Narnia it is rather different. Some of the pictures of Father Christmas in our world make him look only funny and jolly. But now that the children actually stood looking at him they didn't find it quite like that. He was so big, and so glad, and so real, that they all became quite still. They felt very glad, but also solemn.

"I've come at last", he said. "She has kept me out for a long time, but I have got in at last. Aslan is on the move. The Witch's magic is weakening."

And Lucy felt running through her that deep shiver of gladness which you only get if you are being solemn and still.

"And now", said Father Christmas, "for your presents. There is a new and better sewing machine for you, Mrs Beaver. I will drop it in your house as I pass."

"If you please, sir", said Mrs Beaver, making a curtsey. "It's locked up."

"Locks and bolts make no difference to me", said Father Christmas. "And as for you, Mr Beaver, when you get home you will find your dam finished and mended and all the leaks stopped and a new sluice-gate fitted."

Mr Beaver was so pleased that he opened his mouth very wide and then found he couldn't say anything at all.

"Peter, Adam's Son", said Father Christmas.

"Here, sir", said Peter.

"These are your presents," was the answer, "and they are tools not toys. The time to use them is perhaps near at hand. Bear them well." With these words he handed to Peter a shield and a sword. The shield was the colour of silver and across it there ramped a red lion, as bright as a ripe strawberry at the moment when you pick it. The hilt of the sword was of gold and it had a sheath and a sword belt and everything it needed, and it was just the right size and weight for Peter to use. Peter was silent and solemn as he received these gifts, for he felt they were a very serious kind of present.

"Susan, Eve's Daughter", said Father Christmas. "These are for you", and he handed her a bow and a quiver full of arrows and a little ivory horn. "You must use the bow only in great need," he said, "for I do not mean you to fight in the

32

battle. It does not easily miss. And when you put this horn to your lips and blow it, then, wherever you are, I think help of some kind will come to you."

Last of all he said, "Lucy, Eve's Daughter", and Lucy came forward. He gave her a little bottle of what looked like glass (but people said afterwards that it was made of diamond) and a small dagger. "In this bottle," he said, "there is a cordial made of the juice of one of the fire-flowers that grow in the mountains of the sun. If you or any of your friends is hurt, a few drops of this will restore them. And the dagger is to defend yourself at great need. For you also are not to be in the battle."

"Why, sir?" said Lucy. "I think – I don't know – but I think I could be brave enough."

"That is not the point", he said. "But battles are ugly when women fight. And now" – here he suddenly looked less grave – "here is something for the moment for you all!" and he brought out (I suppose from the big bag at his back, but nobody quite saw him do it) a large tray containing five cups and saucers, a bowl of lump sugar, a jug of cream, and a great big teapot all sizzling and piping hot. Then he cried out "Merry Christmas! Long live the true King!" and cracked his whip, and he and the reindeer and the sledge and all were out of sight before anyone realized that they had started.

Peter had just drawn his sword out of its sheath and was showing it to Mr Beaver, when Mrs Beaver said:

"Now then, now then! Don't stand talking there till the tea's got cold. Just like men. Come and help to carry the tray down and we'll have breakfast. What a mercy I thought of bringing the bread-knife."

So down the steep bank they went and back to the cave, and Mr Beaver cut some of the bread and ham into sandwiches, and Mrs Beaver poured out the tea, and everyone enjoyed themselves. But long before they had finished enjoying themselves Mr Beaver said, "Time to be moving on now."

Keeping Christmas

How will you your Christmas keep?
Feasting, fasting, or asleep?
Will you laugh or will you pray,
Or will you forget the day?

Be it kept with joy or prayer,
Keep of either some to spare;
Whatsoever brings the day,
Do not keep but give away.

Eleanor Farjeon

Carol Singing
from A Child's Christmas in Wales

DYLAN THOMAS

Dylan Thomas was born in 1914, the son of a schoolmaster. He worked as a newspaper reporter before becoming a well-known poet and writer. In A Child's Christmas in Wales *he remembers what it was like to grow up in Wales in the 1920s.*

And I remember that we went
singing carols once, when there wasn't the shaving
of a moon to light the flying streets. At the end
of a long road was a drive that led to a large
house, and we stumbled up the darkness of the drive
that night, each one of us afraid, each one holding
a stone in his hand in case, and all of us too brave
to say a word. The wind through the trees
made noises as of old and unpleasant and maybe
webfooted men wheezing in caves. We reached
the black bulk of the house.
"What shall we give them? Hark the Herald?"
"No," Jack said, "Good King Wenceslas.
I'll count three."
One, two, three, and we began to sing,
our voices high and seemingly distant in the
snow-felted darkness round the house that
was occupied by nobody we knew. We stood
close together, near the dark door.
*"Good King Wenceslas looked out
On the Feast of Stephen . . ."*
And then a small, dry voice
of someone who has not spoken for a long time,

joined our singing: a small, dry eggshell voice
from the other side of the door: a small dry voice
through the keyhole. And when we stopped running
we were outside *our* house; the front room was lovely;
balloons floated under the hot-water-bottle-gulping gas;
everything was good again and shone over the town.
"Perhaps it was a ghost", Jim said.
"Perhaps it was trolls", Dan said,
who was always reading.
"Let's go in and see if there's any jelly left",
Jack said. And we did that.

Always on Christmas night there was music.
An uncle played the fiddle, a cousin sang
"Cherry Ripe", and another uncle sang "Drake's Drum".
It was very warm in the little house.
Auntie Hannah, who had got on to the parsnip
wine, sang a song about Bleeding Hearts and Death,
and then another in which she said her heart
was like a Bird's Nest; and then everybody
laughed again; and then I went to bed.
Looking through my bedroom window, out into
the moonlight and the unending smoke-coloured snow,
I could see the lights in the windows
of all the other houses on our hill and hear
the music rising from them up the long, steadily
falling night. I turned the gas down, I got
into bed. I said some words to the close and
holy darkness, and then I slept.

We Three Kings

JANET McNEILL

*No one in the school had wanted to do a nativity play.
From the moment Mr Bingham chose the cast, Dan and
the others had known it would be a flop. But then Jason
Jonson took over as producer, and suddenly the play
began to come unexpectedly to life – until the vicious
Wreckers arrived and destroyed everything the night
before the performance. Dan knew the play must go on,
but now it would have to be held in the afternoon and in
Big Joe's barn . . .*

"Two o'clock!" Dan's Mum declared. "I never heard of such a
thing!" She was swilling the dinner dishes through the hot
soapy water like fury. A jungle of saucepans and bowls,
rolling pin, chopping board – she baked every Saturday
morning after she'd done the shopping – waited at her elbow.
Cutlery lay jumbled in a greasy heap until she was ready to
deal with it. "Two o'clock! It's crazy! Nobody'll ever make it
by two o'clock, you wouldn't expect them. And up in Big Joe's
barn at this time of year! They'll catch their deaths!"

The last of the dinner plates had been washed. Mum
changed the water in the basin and threw in the cutlery noisily
to show her contempt for the alteration in plans.

"That's when it's to be anyway", Dan said dispiritedly. He
ought to have expected it would be like this, but he had been
carried along by the urgent need to perform this play which
had infected them all.

Dad was tying his shoes, his best shoes, making sure the
laces lay straight and even, the way he used to tie them for
church on Sundays, or in the evenings long ago when he and
Mum went out visiting. Did this mean – ? "It would need to

be two o'clock because of the light", Dad said, as if Mum would have to have it explained to her.

"If you'd told me sooner," Mum moaned, "I might have made plans. But coming home as late as this and springing it on me – "

"I couldn't get home to tell you any sooner, Mum. We've been at it all morning in the barn, setting up the bales of hay and putting things right."

The boys had made a good job of the barn. They had built low walls of hay bales along the unwalled side, leaving only sufficient space for the audience to enter. They had set more bales in a semicircle around the area where the choir and the recorder players would be stationed and where the action would take place. Another couple of rows of bales had been added to provide seats for senior spectators, everyone else would have to sit on the ground. The donkeys, puzzled and nervous with all this activity, had withdrawn in a huddle to the field's farther corner.

Meanwhile the girls had scattered to visit any household in the town which might not otherwise have heard the news, and Mrs Hutchin had put up a notice in the window of the Post Office – "School Play – Two o'clock – Up in Big Joe's barn." The news had been passed on by the postman, by bus conductors, in shops and in the barber's, and Mr Hibbert had toured the outlying villages on his motor-bike, taking the school loudhailer with him. The Oldies had persuaded Matron to provide lunch half an hour early instead of changing the time of tea. Big Joe's barn? Yes, they would come, of course they would. Rugs and mufflers, lined boots, hoods and excitement would defeat the weather. They would certainly be there. The members of the school who were to have attended the dress rehearsal would be able to crowd in and find places on the wide floor of the barn, in front of the seated audience. There would be room for everybody.

"You won't need to keep a place for me, that's one sure thing", Mum said, reaching for the washing-up liquid again.

"By the time I've got this lot sorted out and the kitchen cleaned the way I clean it it will be past four, if I know anything about it."

A train went by, the kitchen was filled with the noise of it, and the washing-up water rocked in the basin. That would be the one thirty-seven. Dan's heart sank lower than ever. Mum seemed to relish the effort that all this disorder offered her, as if by putting her kitchen back to its neat immaculate self she proved something, something that was important to her.

"How could I walk out on all this?" she challenged him.

How could she? "I'll have to go on then", Dan said. He knew it was hopeless.

Surprisingly Dad spoke. "We may as well come with you, Dan. Fetch your hat and coat, Doris."

Mum gaped across her confusion of implements and the kitchen that showed up a day's traffic. "I told you. I can't come!"

"You're coming." Dad wasn't asking, he was telling her.

"And leave things in this state? What are you talking about, some women might, but not me. I'd never enjoy a moment of it, you know I wouldn't. And I can read all about it in the paper afterwards, and Dan and you can tell me."

"Hurry now and fetch your things. We've barely got twenty minutes."

Dan's mother lifted her hands out of the hot water and they dripped and steamed while she stared at her husband. It seemed as if she couldn't believe that he was speaking to her like this. Dan could hardly believe it either. His heart ached for Mum to come. Remember what I told you about Baboushka. Of course you must come! Think of Baboushka. Don't let your chance slip away as hers had done.

Still looking at Dad Mum walked to the towel that hung behind the door and dried her hands on it slowly. Then she smiled at him and went off into the bedroom.

"You'd best get on ahead", Dad said to Dan. "I'll see to it that your Mum and I are up in good time."

And Dan, with his heart full of joy and miracles cartwheeling on all sides of him, went on up to school by himself.

Before two o'clock everyone had arrived in Big Joe's barn and the play was ready to begin. They had come in cars, on foot, on bicycles, a couple of taxis, a minibus. The whole of the neighbourhood was there.

Mr Jason Jonson, with humble pride, spoke the prologue and asked the audience to join in singing with the choir the first of the carols.

> "O come, all ye faithful,
> Joyful and triumphant,
> Come ye, o come ye, to Bethlehem."

Bethlehem was in the barn in Big Joe's field. Players and audience stood up to sing and then the play began.

The first scene was the bringing of the news to Mary by the Angel Gabriel. No one needed to be told that Pete was the Angel Gabriel. He had all the authority and dignity of his office. Of course he was the Angel Gabriel, who else could he have been?

> "In Bethlehem's city, in Jewry it was,
> That Joseph and Mary together did pass,
> All for to be taxed when thither they came,
> For Caesar Augustus commanded the same.
> But when they had come to the city so fair
> A number of people so mighty was there
> That Joseph and Mary, whose substance was small
> Could find in the inn there no lodging at all."

Here were the thronged streets of Bethlehem. Here were the tired travellers turned away from the inn, looking for refuge in a stable.

> "Their lodging so simple they took it no scorn,
> And against the next morning our Saviour was born!"

Here was the stable. Now the child had been laid in the manger, Mary and Joseph rested beside him.

Now it was the turn of the recorders with the Pastoral Symphony. Every note was true. Moonlight shone and shivered on the grass of the hillsides around Bethlehem. And there were the shepherds, tending their sheep, with the night sky darkening above them.

> *"Hark the herald angels sing*
> *Glory to the newborn King!"*

Suddenly one angel and then all the company of angels had come with their joyful news. The spectators knew that their unseen wings and haloes were a hundred times more beautiful than anything plastic or gilt paint could ever have produced. Their glory filled Big Joe's barn. The shepherds bent their heads and shielded their eyes from the light.

> *"Say, ye holy shepherds say*
> *What your joyful news today?*
> *Wherefore have you left your sheep*
> *On the lonely mountain steep?"*

The shepherds had come with great joy and had found Mary and Joseph, and the young child lying in a manger.

> *"We three Kings of Orient are,*
> *Bearing gifts we traverse afar,*
> *Field and fountain, moor and mountain,*
> *Following yonder star."*

Caspar, Baltazar and Melchior had alighted from their camels and advanced with their pages in attendance to offer gifts to the child. Plainly the gifts they had brought were kings' gifts, fit for a king. They knelt, Caspar the magnificent, Baltazar the mysterious, Melchior, old, wise and frail, undoubted kings, paying tribute.

41

The play was nearly over now, but the players knew that they had been building a bridge, a bridge between themselves and the little kids squatting wide-eyed in the front row, between themselves and the rest of the school crowded in behind, between themselves and the Mums and Dads who were joining in the choruses of the carols, between themselves and the Oldies, huddled in hoods and scarves, with rugs slung across their shoulders, watching with solemn joy.

And the name of the bridge was Christmas. Christmas had come because the children were there and children will always bring Christmas.

"Ding dong merrily on high,
In heaven the bells are ringing."

And ding dong merrily in Big Joe's barn from angels, shepherds, kings, pages, the recorders going full blast, the music master with the glockenspiel beating out the bells.

Outside the barn the winter afternoon had begun to fade. The donkeys had come to the entrance and stood thrusting inquisitive noses across the bales of hay, nudging each other and jostling. The child in the manger whimpered, and Megan, who had become Mary, leaned forward to pull the shawl a little more closely around him.

Kids' Quotes

Christmas comes so that we can have peace, love and hope all year round.

Julie-Ann, age 7

Christmas makes me friendly. Christmas makes me cosy.

Sadia, age 7

When it is Christmas you must be very kind and you must be sharing.

Matthew, age 6

Christmas is really special because Jesus was born on Christmas Eve and Jesus is really special too.

Nicola, age 7

Jesus is the king of the world. When the people saw Jesus in the stable they thought he was the king of the world too.

Neil, age 7

Jesus was the king of the world and he still is.

Dennis, age 7

At Christmas I think about poor old Santa who gets soot on him.

Claire, age 7

On Christmas Day it was Jesus's birthday and Christmas Day is about love because it is when people celebrate meals.

Julie, age 7

Christmas is a loving day.

Angela, age 8

I like Christmas because you celebrate. You love each other. And it is Jesus's birthday. And you hope that you get the presents.

Paul, age 7

Father Christmas comes from the moon.

Jay, age 5

When I go to bed I hear Jesus calling but it is my Mum. You get toys, people go to the church and have tea.

Christine, age 7

2

Love Came Down at Christmas

God's Wonderful Gift

✠

Mary got ready and hurried off to a town in the hill-country of Judaea. She went into Zechariah's house and greeted Elizabeth. When Elizabeth heard Mary's greeting, the baby moved within her. Elizabeth was filled with the Holy Spirit and said in a loud voice, "You are the most blessed of all women, and blessed is the child you will bear! Why should this great thing happen to me, that my Lord's mother comes to visit me? For as soon as I heard your greeting, the baby within me jumped with gladness. How happy you are to believe that the Lord's message to you will come true!"

Mary said,

"My heart praises the Lord;
my soul is glad because of God my Saviour,
for he has remembered me, his lowly servant!
From now on all people will call me happy,
because of the great things the Mighty God
has done for me.
His name is holy;
from one generation to another
he shows mercy to those who honour him.
He has stretched out his mighty arm
and scattered the proud with all their plans.
He has brought down mighty kings
from their thrones,
and lifted up the lowly.
He has filled the hungry with good things,
and sent the rich away with empty hands.
He has kept the promise he made to our ancestors,
and has come to the help of his servant Israel.
He has remembered to show mercy to Abraham
and to all his descendants for ever!"

Mary stayed about three months with Elizabeth and then went back home.

(Luke 1:39–56)

✠

It's All In the Name

RICHARD BEWES

Smith might be thought of as a common name, particularly in the West, but the Changs take the all-time top prize. There are seventy-five million of them! Here and there special and even unique names are created out of peculiar circumstances associated with the person's birth – Anaesthesia was the name given to the first baby born with the help of chloroform. A Kenyan, born in the back of a Ford V8 car in the 1940s, was christened Motoka, while there is a Ugandan today whose parents gave him the prestigious name of Oxford University Press.

There was one baby, however, whose arrival was so epoch-making that he was being given his distinctive title-names over seven hundred years before he was born. The ripples and reverberations were spreading on *both* sides of his birth. We have to admit that the names were unique:

And he will be called Wonderful Counsellor, Mighty God, Everlasting Father, Prince of Peace. (NIV)

Isaiah, like other Old Testament prophets, had the God-given ability of standing at the point where two worlds touched – the transcendent and the ordinary, the eternal and the historical – and of interpreting the one to the other. It was not for the prophet to give the *full* picture, just the essentials were necessary. So the name Jesus was not spelt out then; in any case, many Jewish mothers would call their babies Jesus (or Joshua) – it was the name for a deliverer.

No, here was someone uniquely a special. The figure that Isaiah could see approaching on the highroads of time was nothing less than a divine person; the government was to be upon his shoulders, and of his kingdom there would be no end. He was to be Master of the World.

If it was Isaiah who got the name right, it was a contemporary of his, Micah, who got the place right:

> But you, Bethlehem Ephrathah, though you are small among the clans of Judah, out of you will come for me one who will be ruler over Israel, whose origins are from old, from ancient times. (NIV)

Like Isaiah, Micah was standing at the point where the two worlds touched – the temporary, but also the timeless. Bethlehem, a nonentity of a town, would be hallowed in songs, carols and oratorios of the future because of the birth that took place there. But the birth only gave the town significance because of the other, the eternal dimension, of this unique individual "whose origins are from old".

It was the prophets who demonstrated conclusively that although the arrival of which they spoke was a one-off happening, it was no mere accident of history. It had been coming for a long time. Here was the culmination of centuries of preparation; here was the pivotal point of history, dividing BC from AD, the birth of a baby in whom two worlds were to touch – the divine and the human. It had all been foreseen hundreds of years earlier.

There is a Chinese fable of a weary traveller (was his name Chang?) journeying through the desert. At last he came upon a great shady oak tree. "At last!" he exclaimed, sinking down to rest under its branches. "How lucky I am to have found you!"

"Lucky?" retorted the oak tree. "It's not luck. I've been waiting for you for the last seven hundred years."

That Early Morning in Bethlehem

JOHN TIMPSON

The story of the first Christmas morning has been told and acted so often in kindergartens and Sunday Schools, yet no two versions are ever quite the same. The basic ingredients are there: the Angel appearing to Mary, the shepherds watching their flocks, the three wise men from Orient far, Joseph and Mary turned away at the inn, the Babe lying in the manger. Yet somehow a six-year-old can manage to provide a totally different interpretation of a familiar role, or adjust the story to suit present-day conceptions. A small child's adaptation of that early morning in Bethlehem, and the events that led up to it and followed it, can be quite disarming. These incidents involving casts and classrooms at Christmastide are all vouched for as authentic by the listeners who sent them in to "Today".

The Rebellious Innkeeper

A small boy was bitterly disappointed at not being cast as Joseph in the school Nativity play. He was given the minor role of the innkeeper instead – and throughout the weeks of rehearsal he brooded on how he could avenge himself on his successful rival.

Came the day of the performance, Joseph and Mary made their entrance and knocked on the door of the inn. The innkeeper opened it a fraction, and eyed them coldly.

"Can you offer us board and lodging for the night?" pleaded Joseph, impeccably following the script. "My wife is soon to have a baby." They stood back, awaiting the expected rebuff.

But the innkeeper had not pondered all those weeks for nothing. To the confusion of the producer and the delight of the audience he flung the door wide, beamed genially at the couple and cried hospitably: "Come in, come in. You are very welcome. You shall have the best room in the hotel."

There was a pause. Then the youthful Joseph displayed the resource and initiative which perhaps got him the part in the first place. With great presence of mind he said to Mary: "Hold on – I'll take a look inside first." He peered ostentatiously past the innkeeper, shook his head firmly and announced: "I'm not taking my wife into a place like that. Come on, Mary, we'll sleep in the stable."

The plot was back on course . . .

And the Exonerated Innkeeper

A Sunday School teacher was telling a group of four- and five-year-olds the story of that Christmas morning, and explaining that Jesus was born in a stable because (regardless of what that mutinous innkeeper may have said) there really was no room at the inn.

A worldly-wise little Yorkshire lad at the back of the class was heard to murmur to his neighbour: "I blame Joseph. He should have booked."

What's In a Name?

Such disconcerting moments can occur quite unintentionally. At a primary school Nativity play in Cheshire it happened even earlier in the performance. The first scene had passed without incident. Mary was told by the Angel that she was blessed by God and would be giving birth to his holy child. Then came Scene Two. Enter Mary and Joseph, chatting.

Mary: "I met this fairy in the garden. He said I'm going to have a baby."

Joseph: "Great! What are you going to call it?"

Mary (totally forgets next line. Then, after thinking hard): "Colin."

Exit Mary stage right, followed by a puzzled Joseph muttering: "Colin Christ?"

Any Odd Jobs in Heaven?

The story of the Annunciation also caused a problem for a cub scout group in the East End of London. A Sister told them the story, ending with Mary's reply to the Angel: "Behold the handmaid of the Lord."

She asked one of the cubs to retell the story in his own words. He went through it very accurately until he came to the last lines, when somehow he managed to replace Mary by Joseph. In his version it was Joseph who answered the Angel, with a slight variation on the original.

"Behold," said Joseph, "behold the handyman of the Lord."

Flights of Fancy

The Flight into Egypt has conjured up some strange images among the very young. A teacher at one primary school told her class the story of the Angel appearing to Joseph in a dream and saying: "Take the young child and his mother, and flee into Egypt." The children were asked to illustrate the story.

One small boy drew Joseph leading the donkey on which Mary was riding. He had the donkey's bridle in one hand, and in the other he carried a walking stick with a large black dot on top.

"What is that meant to be?" asked the teacher, pointing to the dot.

"That's the flea", he explained.

Another child in another class, but depicting the same subject, came up with a more modernistic approach. For the flight into Egypt he actually drew an aeroplane. There were four figures discernible inside.

The teacher decided to make the best of it. "Very nice", she said. "I can see Joseph and Mary and Jesus – but who is the one in front?"

The little lad looked at her proudly. "That's Pontius the Pilot," he said.

Christmas in Israel

WALTER BARKER

Israel is a land where three religions meet. Christians, Jews and Moslems all regard Jerusalem as a holy city, and Palestine, historically, has been a holy land to the adherents of all. It is therefore a land with constant religious festivals taking place and sometimes overlapping. Different varieties of Christians keep Christmas at different times. The Western Christmas comes first on 25th December, followed by the Greek Orthodox about a week later, and finally the Armenians a week after that. The festival therefore seems to go on for ever.

With Bethlehem only five miles from Jerusalem, and the suburbs of each city growing together, one has hardly left the built-up part of Jerusalem before one arrives at the birthplace of Christ. The weather is cool with the possibility of rain. At 3,000 feet above sea level the winds can be bitingly cold, although if the sun shines they are tempered somewhat. It hardly ever snows in Jerusalem at Christmas, and the earth is never "as hard as iron", to quote the well-known carol. Even in January, the middle of winter, hard frosts are very rare.

Most of the indigenous Christians in Israel are of Arab background and belong to the Eastern Churches, and they flock to worship in Bethlehem at Christmas. Sad to say, because of the security situation and the possibility of terrorist action, the town is full of heavily-armed soldiers. The Church of the Nativity, said to be built on the birthplace of Christ, is of course Bethlehem's most famous landmark. It actually consists of two churches, one Greek Orthodox and the other Latin (Roman Catholic). Christmas night means long processions and long services but is an experience. The church is packed with Christians of different persuasions, and the clergy, dressed in their vestments according to their denomination, carry out a grand ritual. The Eastern Christians believe in spectacle, lights, colour: not for them the drabness of much Protestant Christianity. The birth of a baby is always regarded as a time of joy, and the midnight service certainly reflects this.

For the Western Christian there are services in the numerous caves and grottoes of the shepherds' fields, within walking distance of the town. Sheep graze outside as services are followed by refreshments in the form of pitta bread filled with bits of roasted lamb. There are also the usual Christmas services in the other churches and a big united service in the YMCA, to which all churches are invited.

In the Christian homes, celebrations take the traditional form according to the community from which the family comes. The constitution of Israel guarantees freedom of religion to all its inhabitants, so the government is anxious to make certain that Christians can observe the festival as they wish. As far as individual Israelis are concerned, many are from Europe and remember Christmas celebrated in their original homeland. There is the story of the little Jewish boy decorating the tree in his home and saying to his father: "Do the Christians keep Christmas like we do?" Carol singing has a special nostalgia for many, and carol services are often crowded, though Jews do not usually attend Christian churches.

Of course, Judaism has its own midwinter festival – Hanukkah. This is the Feast of Dedication mentioned in the Gospel of John (10:22). About a hundred and fifty years before the birth of Christ, the Jews in Palestine faced a crisis – an attack on their religion by the then rulers of Syria, which included Judaea. Antiochus Epiphanes ruled, and in order to unify his domains tried to destroy the Jewish faith which then, as throughout history, aimed at separating the Jews from surrounding Gentile culture. This attack involved desecrating the Temple. There was a rebellion, led by a family called the

Maccabees, which resulted in the defeat of the Syrians and a short time of independence for Jews.

Hanukkah is observed in honour of the reconsecration of the Temple. Tradition has it that a one-day supply of oil for the Temple lasted the eight days of the feast, allowing the dedication to proceed without any need for more oil to be made ready. So the festival lasts eight days, and a nine-branch candlestick is put in full view in the window. The first day, one candle is lit with the ninth candle. The second day, two are lit and so on through eight days. Gifts are given and parties are held. The first day of the festival is the twenty-fifth of the Jewish month Kislev. This does not often coincide with 25th December, but it is interesting that about the same time as Jews are lighting their Hanukkah candles, Christians celebrate the arrival of the one they believe is the light of the world!

> Love came down at Christmas,
> Love all lovely, Love Divine;
> Love was born at Christmas,
> Star and angels gave the sign.
>
> Worship we the Godhead,
> Love Incarnate, Love Divine;
> Worship we our Jesus:
> But wherewith for sacred sign?
>
> Love shall be our token,
> Love be yours and love be mine,
> Love to God and all men,
> Love for plea and gift and sign.

Michael Bourdeaux

The following is an extract from a sermon preached in January 1963 by the late Archpriest Vsevolod Shpiller. It illustrates the faith and teaching of the Orthodox Church in the Soviet Union, and I find it both moving and simple.

About Christmas and Easter

In spirit the eyes of Orthodox Christians today are once again fixed on the picture of the divine Child in the manger at Bethlehem. Before him kneel the wise men with their gifts of love and wisdom of all ages; above shines the star which has shown them the way, while the angels bend down to earth and praise God.

How we long to see this star in the sky today! It is so difficult to find the way to the manger by electric light! We would like to kneel at the manger with the shepherds and the wise men in order to share in the joy of Christmas. For we know how great that joy is!

Our earthly joys pass and are gone, and how often do they end in pain and distress. But the joy of Christmas (we are told), the joy proclaimed by the angels, will never pass away (John 16:22). No one can take it from us either in this life or the next.

In the midst of modern life, how often do we stand confused, overwhelmed by the changes, the naked facts and the old mysteries which remain unsolved. We cannot find our place in this world. One explanation presents itself: that we belong to Christ, whereas the world is not Christian and does not want to be. What seems to us to be a fact is regarded by many people only as a dilemma: either to accept the de-Christianized world and adapt oneself to it, or else to withdraw from it and reject it as strange and hostile to our way of thinking and feeling.

The joy of Christmas saves us from this dilemma. No explosion of nuclear weapons under the earth or up in the infinite realms of space can drown the Gospel words, "The Word was made flesh" (John 1:14). "The Word was God. The same was in the beginning with God. All things were made by him . . . In him was life; and the life was the light of men" (John 1:1–4). This Word entered the created world for all in the miracle of the incarnation. This marks the centre of the culmination of the creation and we know that nothing in the world can alter the fact: "In this was manifested the love of God toward us, because that God sent his only begotten Son into the world, that we might live through him" (1 John 4:9). This infinite love cannot be withdrawn, nor can that which it has bestowed upon us.

Let us banish the thought of death. The idea of death and the thought of his own inevitable ends fills man with sadness. Is death the end of everything that we love, everything that we cherish in ourselves and in others, all the values, everything by which the soul lives? If all this were to end in the terrible emptiness of the grave, life would be emptied of all value, because this void may open at any moment. Involuntarily our imagination pictures total annihilation (for me death will be the end of everything) and all our joys are destroyed by the picture of death.

But God became man. His incarnation is the beginning of the liberation of all men and of the whole creation from the power of death . . . .

Adrian Snell

In writing our musical, *The Virgin*, we wanted to look with fresh eyes not at the tinselly side of Christmas but at the raw realities of the implications surrounding the birth of the Messiah. We were seeking to portray the struggles and traumas surrounding God's call on Mary to fulfil his plan with her "help", and also the pain and confusion caused in Joseph's life. This song of Mary's tells of what we imagine she may have felt and thought when the angel told her she would give birth to the Messiah.

How Can I Explain?

How can I explain?
I have the universe within me,
I carry love
As it has never been known.
How can I explain?
He won't believe in angels,
I'll just be labelled as someone to disown.
How can I explain?
My love is still the same.

So much to explain.
There must be a way to tell him,
Yet what shall I say
If the shame is all he sees?
How can I explain
The way the Lord has touched me?

Where shall I find the words
That will put his mind at ease?
How can I explain?
My love is still the same.

So much for all our plans.
Seems it's all going to change,
Yet I don't know how.
Will he share my joy, will he understand
That I need his love more than ever now?
Oh, I know it won't be easy,
I can just see his face when I tell him.
Will he still love me through the shame?
All I can say is my love is still the same.

Phil Thomson

David Winter

In Luke's story, the Holy Spirit "came upon" Mary. The resulting conception was both human and divine; and the baby who resulted from it was human and divine: not, as is sometimes suggested, half human and half divine, but fully both, a perfect fusion – as every baby is – of the characteristics of both parents. So Jesus becomes the perfect Saviour for the human race. He is divine (on his Father's side, as we might say) and so can perfectly represent God to the human race. He is human (on his mother's side) and so can perfectly represent us to God. He "understands" God and he "understands" us. Through him, true communication can take place.

No Room at the Inn

STUART JACKMAN

Midnight on Christmas Eve is magic – a time for ghosts. When the clocks strike twelve they hammer a hole in time and eternity slips silently through.

So I was not really surprised to feel a sudden chill in the room and to see him sitting there opposite me beside the dying fire. He was in his fifties. Shrewd dark eyes, smooth black hair. And the well-groomed charm of the good hotelier. I had never seen him before but knew, immediately, who he was.

"Cold night", I said.

He stretched his hand towards the fire, so real that it was difficult to believe he existed only in my mind. "Very cold", he said. "And I was dog-tired. Out on my feet with the beginnings of a migraine." He looked at me quickly. "I'm not making excuses – don't think that – just trying to explain how it was."

I nodded, watching him settle more comfortably into the chair. "We were coining money, I'm not denying that", he said. "Some high-grade civil servant with his eye on the New Year's honours list dreams up this idea of a census. It's inconvenient, of course. Right in the middle of winter, everything frozen up solid, the roads like glaciers. No time to be trekking round the country to sign on the dotted line in your old home town. But it was money in the bank for us.

"We're just a small country inn. Nothing fancy, no frills. A friendly welcome, clean beds, good home-cooked country fare. Most years we just about break even. But we had more people through the place in that one week than we normally get in six months. I'd have been a fool not to cash in on it."

He brooded silently for a moment or two, staring into the fire. When he looked up his eyes were haunted. "She was a

60

nice little thing with shy, gentle eyes. Very young and very pregnant. Her husband was older. Big chap, a bit rough and ready, with an accent you could hang your hat on. But basically a decent sort. I took to them straightaway. If I'd had a room they'd have been more than welcome to it." He leaned forward, his voice suddenly sharp. "And that's the honest truth."

"Of course", I said. "But you were full."

"Full?" he said. "You've said it. Shared rooms, beds on the landing – we even had people sleeping on two chairs in the public rooms. Paying through the nose and glad to do it." He shook his head. "He offered me double the going rate. The husband, I mean. But it wasn't a question of money. The way they were placed I'd put them up for free. On the house, no problem. There was something about them you don't often see. A kind of innocence. Something – I can't explain it – something different. Special." He smiled, a small, wry smile. "That's when I should have guessed what it was all about, I suppose. But I didn't."

There was a little pause, heavy with regret.

I said gently, "So you put them in the stable."

He nodded. "It was my wife's idea. I was against it at first. After all, we've got our reputation to think of, and sleeping guests in a stable isn't exactly going to get us four-star rating, is it? But my wife can be very stubborn and my head was pounding and I was too bushed to argue.

"So we took them round the back and settled them in among the horses and the old wagon ox, with a pile of blankets and a bale of clean straw. I'm not saying it was comfortable but at least it was dry and out of the weather. My wife brought them hot soup and a loaf fresh from the oven and they were grateful." His face tightened. "That's what gets me", he said thickly. "They were so grateful. So damned grateful." He hesitated and cleared his throat. "Well, we didn't charge them of course", he said, as if offering a plea of mitigation.

"What about the shepherds?"

"Yes, well, the shepherds came", he said. "Nothing unusual about that. This time of the year we always leave the back door on the latch and a jug or two of mulled wine on the hob. It's cold work keeping sheep out in the open in winter, and the shepherds often come down in twos and threes for a bit of a warm. Take it in turns, you see? But that night they all came together. Just before dawn it was. I heard them milling about in the yard and got up to see what the excitement was, and that's when I discovered the baby had been born.

"There must've been about a dozen of them all crowded into the stable just staring at the baby. When I told my wife she was horrified. I wasn't too pleased myself. It's bad enough giving birth on a heap of straw – no doctor, no midwife – without having half the village come barging in on you. Doesn't do a lot for our image either. Not what you'd call good publicity. They usually come very quietly – the shepherds, I mean. But not that night."

"Been at the mulled wine, had they?" I said.

"That's what I thought", he said. "But it wasn't that. I wish it had been, but it wasn't. They were – I don't know – frightened out of their wits and at the same time wildly happy. Babbling away about angels and a star and a voice in the sky telling them God had been born in my stable. I didn't believe a word of it, of course. Well, who would? I mean, if God decided to get himself born – and that seemed to me to be pretty unlikely – he'd choose the palace in Jerusalem, wouldn't he? Not my stable.

"My wife agreed. She reckoned it was just a story the shepherds had made up. A sort of alibi to cover themselves for abandoning the sheep like that. They'd all come, you see. Normally they'd never do that."

He shook his head. "But then, later in the week, these three VIPs arrive out of nowhere and ask to see the five-day-old king. I was worried then, all right. Scared, too.

They were educated men. Scholars." He spread his hands. "Men like that don't make up crazy stories. I was just relieved we had the young family in the hotel by then. Moved them in the day the baby was born. Some people left after breakfast and we switched things round a bit. Best room in the house and still no charge."

"A nice gesture", I said.

"Too little, too late", he said. "God came knocking on my door and I turned him away."

"An understandable mistake," I said, "in the circumstances. But you made up for it afterwards."

He nodded doubtfully. "I just wish I could believe it was enough."

"I think he would think so," I said.

*

My wife appeared in her dressing-gown. "Are you all right?" she said. "I thought I heard voices. Did someone come in?"

I looked at the empty chair. "No. I was just talking to myself."

"Oh", she said uncertainly. "What about?"

"Forgiveness", I said. "Merry Christmas, love."

The Archbishop of Canterbury

"Advent 1955" by John Betjeman is one of my favourite Christmas poems. I admire its mixture of pathos and humour, and am always captivated by the sense of excitement and expectation it generates: not so much for "the sweet and silly Christmas things" as for the real heart of Christmas – "the birth of God made Man for us on earth". Indeed, the poem's final lines contain all the theology we need to appreciate the moving and miraculous point and purpose of Christmas:

> Yet if God had not given so
> He still would be a distant stranger
> And not the Baby in the manger.

Advent 1955

The Advent wind begins to stir
With sea-like sounds in our Scotch fir,
It's dark at breakfast, dark at tea,
And in between we only see
Clouds hurrying across the sky
And rain-wet roads the wind blows dry
And branches bending to the gale
Against great skies all silver-pale.
The world seems travelling into space,
And travelling at a faster pace
Than in the leisured summer weather
When we and it sit out together,
For now we feel the world spin round
On some momentous journey bound –

Journey to what? to whom? to where?
The Advent bells call out "Prepare,
Your world is journeying to the birth
Of God made Man for us on earth."

And how, in fact, do we prepare
For the great day that waits us there –
The twenty-fifth day of December,
The birth of Christ? For some it means
An interchange of hunting scenes
On coloured cards. And I remember
Last year I sent out twenty yards,
Laid end to end, of Christmas cards
To people that I scarcely know –
They'd sent a card to me, and so
I had to send one back, Oh dear!
Is this a form of Christmas cheer?
Or is it, which is less surprising,
My pride gone in for advertising?
The only cards that really count
Are that extremely small amount
From real friends who keep in touch
And are not rich but love us much.
Some ways indeed are very odd
By which we hail the birth of God.

We raise the price of things in shops,
We give plain boxes fancy tops
And lines which traders cannot sell
Thus parcell'd go extremely well.
We dole out bribes we call a present
To those to whom we must be pleasant
For business reasons. Our defence is
These bribes are charged against expenses
And bring relief in Income Tax.
Enough of these unworthy cracks!

"The time draws near the birth of Christ",
A present that cannot be priced
Given two thousand years ago.
Yet if God had not given so
He still would be a distant stranger
And not the Baby in the manger.

John Betjeman

Roy Castle

My favourite Christmas carol is "In the Bleak Mid-winter".

In the bleak mid-winter,
Frosty wind made moan,
Earth stood hard as iron,
Water like a stone;
Snow had fallen, snow on snow,
Snow on snow,
In the bleak mid-winter,
Long ago.

Our God, heaven cannot hold him,
Nor earth sustain;
Heaven and earth shall flee away
When he comes to reign:
In the bleak mid-winter
A stable-place sufficed
The Lord God Almighty,
Jesus Christ.

Angels and archangels
May have gathered there,
Cherubim and seraphim
Thronged the air;

But his mother only,
In her maiden bliss,
Worshipped the Beloved
With a kiss.

What can I give him,
Poor as I am?
If I were a shepherd,
I would bring a lamb;
If I were a wise man,
I would do my part;
Yet what I can I give him –
Give my heart.

Christmas

NORMAN ST JOHN-STEVAS

Christmas is both a pagan and a Christian celebration, but we should not be disturbed by this. Grace builds on nature. The feasting, the giving and receiving of presents, the reunions with family and friends, the imaginative and moving picture of the child in the stable watched over by the ox and the ass and visited by the three kings, are all things good in themselves, but in the light of the Incarnation they are lifted up and transformed into a lasting joy.

The Christian is at all times two-world-centred but at certain moments more obviously so than at others. Christmas is one of these. The greatness of Christmas is that it is a supreme moment of interpenetration of one world by the other. We stand in adoration and awe before the crib, recalling the moment when the Almighty, the God of majesty and power, the creator and sustainer of the universe, stooped down towards the world which he made and reduced himself to that most helpless of creatures, a new-born babe. In that embodiment of gift and condescension and love, we get a glimpse of what God is really like, a being whose nature it is to love and who can do no other. At Christmas that fiery furnace is transubstantiated into the gentleness, the meekness and helplessness of a tiny child.

In the Christian cosmology there stands God and there stands man, bearing the burden of his individuality for ever. The Incarnation brings the two together. The difference between them is that he is sinless and men are steeped in sin, subject to pride and selfishness and lust – and not only their own but also the accumulated sinfulness of the human race. Mankind is caught in the structures of sin, in the Church, in the State, in individual lives, unable to free themselves save through the mediation of that child. Without Jesus the whole human race, individually and collectively, is trapped by sin: but this is the child who lifts the intolerable burden from mankind and carries it from him, who bears the burden of guilt and evil on his own shoulders and who in the end will carry it, actually, in the form of the Cross. Even as the Wise Men hasten towards Bethlehem filled with indescribable joy by the sight of the star, as Matthew tells us, the shadow and the glory of the Cross are seen in the stable where the child lies, the child who has come to save his people from their sins.

From that moment, the great work of redemption is set in motion, redemption not only of the individual but also of the whole human race. It is the race, and not the individuals alone who compose it, that is to be saved. The theology of redemption highlights the evil of racialism, which implicitly denies it. And in this work of redemption, so secretly and humbly set in motion, every individual has his or her part to play, so that in the end the new creation, described by St Paul, comes to fruition. So the Church is right at Christmas to give thanks for this greatest of gifts of God to man, to bid us fall to our knees in adoration and praise in the stable filled with the light of that heavenly child.

Merry Christmas, Nicole

PATRICIA ANN FISHER

It was Christmas Eve, a typical California Christmastime with fingers of fog pushing aside the bushes surrounding the house and cautiously peeping into the room filled with the disarray of the season. Choosing to ignore the disorderly room, I peered through fog and falling dusk to watch an approaching car. As the porch light cast an eerie welcome, the vehicle crept slowly to the curb where its engine shuddered into silence.

The car door opened and an unfamiliar figure emerged, gingerly carrying a bulky package. I opened the door quickly and greeted a rosy-cheeked replica of Santa without the fringe benefits of beard and suit.

"Hi, I'm Greg Adams and this is Nicole", he announced as the bundle in his arms began to cry. Looking around at the Christmas decor, he smiled as he handed the baby to me. "She's just in time for Christmas."

I peeled back the blanket as I took the baby whose cries were now screams. She squinted at me with terror and suspicion, her little body rigid in my arms. Speaking soothingly, I said, "It's all right, Nicole, you're home now; no one is going to hurt you." She halted in mid-scream, eyed me with all the apprehension of a six-month-old sceptic, and continued to scream with unwavering intensity.

"Well, I guess you've heard babies scream before", Mr. Adams quipped, simultaneously glancing at his watch with impatience.

"Plenty of times," I admitted, "but I've never heard such a cry of agony." I clasped the child closely, trying with little success to comfort her.

"She's still terrified", he conceded. "She weighed seven

pounds at birth and only nine at the hospital just now, so she's more than a little undernourished. The bruises aren't much, at least the ones we can see. Those marks around her mouth are from her grandmother's hand. Guess they really tried to turn the kid off. Both the mother and grandmother. Lucky for the kid, they have nosy neighbours. Well, thanks for taking her; I know I didn't give you much warning." Consulting his watch again, he muttered, "I gotta go. Merry Christmas!"

"Merry Christmas", I responded weakly, but he was already closing the door.

"Well, Nicole, two pounds in six months. Either you don't like to eat or someone doesn't like to feed you." I cuddled her closely to me, but her body remained rigid and the howling persisted. *Ann*, I told myself, *you did it this time, trekked all the way to Bethlehem without benefit of the star.*

My attention was temporarily diverted from Nicole's screams as the headlights of our elderly station wagon penetrated the fog, pinpointing the driveway with practised ease. I heard the car doors slam and the cheerful voices of my family giggling with pre-Christmas anticipation as they rushed the front door. They halted in unison in the hallway, staring and silent. *They are definitely and absolutely neither shepherds nor wisemen. Maybe sheep, though*, I pondered tentatively. Nicole, unaware of the intruders, continued to yell.

"What is that?" demanded fourteen-year-old Matt.

"This is called a baby", I explained with exaggerated patience.

"Where'd we get it? How long is it going to stay? Does it cry all the time?" asked thirteen-year-old Lisa who knew enough in a family of seven not to mince questions.

"Her name is Nicole; we'll have her as long as she needs us; and I think she *does* cry all the time."

"We leave you one hour on Christmas Eve and look what happens", lamented sixteen-year-old Laura in her eldest child's patronizing tone. "Looks like we're doing mangers this year." I didn't tell her that I'd had exactly the same thought.

"Here, let me take her." I could always trust David to have a practical suggestion. "I've had a little experience", he twinkled.

"Five kids is not what I'd call experience", Laura added. "Most people learn from experience." She flounced to her room. *She'll have one absolutely perfect child*, I thought. As a baby she even burped neatly. As a toddler she made perfect mud pies, and her first day of kindergarten she conquered the school system. Now we could count on her being unerring in any argument – or at least on being able to convince the others of her invincibility.

Meanwhile, experience was not helping David, so I decided on the warm-bottle approach. Julie and Jill, our eight-year-old twins, followed me to the kitchen.

"So, this is what you've kept these baby bottles for", commented Jill.

Not wanting to destroy a child's illusions at Christmas, I merely smiled. There was no reason for her to know I hadn't cleaned the cupboards in eight years. Big-eyed, Jill and Julie marvelled at my expertise in pouring milk from a carton to a bottle and then warming it.

Unimpressed, David yelled, "Lost the knack, honey? Hurry, this kid wants to eat. She must be starved!"

Testing a drop of milk on my arm for temperature, I handed the bottle to David. Expertly, he inserted the nipple into the baby's mouth. She sucked greedily, and David gave me his "it-takes-someone-who-knows" smile. At that moment Nicole abruptly stopped sucking and began to howl again.

"I guess I could change her", I suggested. "Lisa, get those baby clothes down from your closet."

Lisa hurried off, "Sure, Mom, they're on the closet floor; they fell down last summer when I was trying to find my swimming suit."

In spite of Nicole's continuing sobs, I smiled. Lisa was a child after my own heart. Quite obviously if the clothes had

71

fallen on the floor, that must be their rightful place. It was, as I called it, the divine right of things.

As I undressed Nicole, we all gasped at our first sight of her tiny, emaciated body. It was a mass of bruises. She shuddered from cold and pain. "Oh, Nikki", I murmured. "I'm so sorry. We won't ever let this happen again, not ever." I dressed her carefully in the softest gown, a remnant of the time long ago when people had given us gifts for having babies.

The children stood together, eyes wide with shock. Even Laura emerged from the sanctuary of her room. "I'll hold her, Mom", she offered softly.

But it was David and I who took turns holding her through that long Christmas Eve, rocking her, loving her, willing her to live. At some point in the night, Nicole reluctantly drank an ounce of milk, at another she slept for half an hour, but mostly she alternately cried, screamed, and yelled.

Just before Christmas dawned, I still held the tiny bundle and whispered lullabies. Matt tiptoed in and stood by the rocking chair. "Mom, Jesus got Christmas gifts, we have nothing for Nicole."

"Oh, yes, we do, Matt. She just doesn't know how to accept our gift yet. It's called *love*", I replied softly.

"How will she learn to accept love?"

"The way you did, Matt, and the way all the others did. You learned to love by being loved. And that's how Nicole will learn too. It will be a little harder for her, though, because she isn't sure if love is real."

And so Nicole cried, unaware of Christmas, unaware of love. She didn't know that her Christmas journey had ended, that she'd found her very own manger.

Lord, you were rich
    beyond all splendour,
yet, for love's sake, became so poor,
leaving your throne
    in glad surrender,
sapphire-paved courts
    for stable floor:
Lord, you were rich
    beyond all splendour,
yet, for love's sake became so poor.

You are our God
    beyond all praising,
yet, for love's sake, became a man;
stooping so low, but sinners raising
heavenwards, by your eternal plan:
you are our God,
    beyond all praising,
yet, for love's sake, became a man.

Lord, you are love
    beyond all telling,
Saviour and king, we worship you;
Emmanuel, within us dwelling,
make us and keep us pure and true:
Lord, you are love
    beyond all telling,
Saviour and king, we worship you.

Frank Houghton

Sheila Walsh

Christmas is a very special time in our family. It seems to be one of the few occasions in the year when we all get together!

Madonna, the singer, said that we live in a "material world" and that's so true. I always try to take some time out in the midst of the crackers, turkey and old movies to remember the greatest act of selflessness displayed on our little planet. When God the Father sent Jesus his Son into the world, he knew that the life he would live would be one ultimately of rejection and pain. Knowing all this, he still sent him. He sent him to all of us, to help us find our way home.

My prayer for each one of us this Christmas would be that more than all the presents we'll receive, we'll take hold of the greatest gift of all.

James Fox

My favourite thing to do with Chistmas is salvation, available to all men.

Arise, shine; for your light has come,
  and the glory of the Lord has risen upon you.
For behold, darkness shall cover the earth,
  and thick darkness the peoples;
but the Lord will arise upon you,
  and his glory will be seen upon you.
And nations shall come to your light,
  and kings to the brightness of your rising.

(Isaiah 60:1–3, RSV)

3

O Come, All Ye Faithful

Christmas Remembered

✠

At that time the Emperor Augustus ordered a census to be taken throughout the Roman Empire. When this first census took place, Quirinius was the governor of Syria. Everyone, then, went to register himself, each to his own town.

Joseph went from the town of Nazareth in Galilee to the town of Bethlehem in Judaea, the birthplace of King David. Joseph went there because he was a descendant of David. He went to register with Mary, who was promised in marriage to him. She was pregnant, and while they were in Bethlehem, the time came for her to have her baby. She gave birth to her first son, wrapped him in strips of cloth and laid him in a manger – there was no room for them to stay in the inn.

There were some shepherds in that part of the country who were spending the night in the fields, taking care of their flocks. An angel of the Lord appeared to them, and the glory of the Lord shone over them. They were terribly afraid, but the angel said to them, "Don't be afraid! I am here with good news for you, which will bring great joy to all the people. This very day in David's town your Saviour was born – Christ the Lord! And this is what will prove it to you: you will find a baby wrapped in strips of cloth and lying in a manger."

Suddenly a great army of heaven's angels appeared with the angel, singing praises to God:

"Glory to God in the highest heaven,
and peace on earth to those with whom he is pleased!"

When the angels went away from them back into heaven, the shepherds said to one another, "Let's go to Bethlehem and see this thing that has happened which the Lord has told us."

So they hurried off and found Mary and Joseph and saw the

baby lying in the manger. When the shepherds saw him, they told them what the angel had said about the child. All who heard were amazed at what the shepherds said.

Mary remembered all these things and thought deeply about them. The shepherds went back, singing praises to God for all they had heard and seen; it had been just as the angel had told them.

(Luke 2:1–20)

Eamonn Andrews

Christmas is a mist of memories for me – all of them happy.
There must have been one or two or three not so happy but
the mist is most obliging. For no reason that I can account
for, the clearest and sharpest memory seems to go back to
when I believed in Santa Claus (still do).

It was family custom that we go to six o'clock Mass on
Christmas morning. It was a short enough walk to the church
of St Teresa, and all I can remember is the darkness and
starlight. It must have rained some Christmas but I don't
remember it. The morning I do remember is the one where
Santa had left in the bottom of my pillowcase the most
treasured of all his gifts, a battery-powered torch. I can still
feel the thrill of being allowed to take it with me to Mass, and
sending the thin white beam all over the streets and the
houses and finally up and up and up until it met one of the
stars.

Nicholas Hinton

From the age of eight to thirteen I sang as a chorister at
Salisbury Cathedral. Christmas was of course one of the
highlights of the year and the choristers were expected to be
on duty – a fact that amazed many people. Fancy depriving
these children of Christmas at home! How wrong they were;
Christmas at the cathedral was wonderful, we were terribly
spoilt as everyone from the bishop downwards felt that
parties, presents and pantomimes had to be provided. The
truth is that Christmas for me has proved relatively dark ever
since.

John Motson

Christmas at boarding school used to have a special feel about it. Pantomimes, parties and end-of-term functions would precede the long-awaited trek home for the holidays and a time of celebration after being away from parents for three months.

I always remember that we had an annual carol service which seemed a focal point on the school calendar. Although Culford was a Methodist school, the Christian message was gently persuasive rather than evangelical. Masters were often lay preachers, and one of them once gave us all a formula for prayer.

Take the word "lofty", he said, because we should always be striving for lofty ideals. Then remember the initial letters, and pray as follows:

L   for the Lord's Prayer
O   for others in time of need
F   for forgiveness for your sins
T   for thanksgiving for all God's gifts
Y   for yourself, last of all.

I have used that theme down the years ever since, and although many of us probably do not pray as often as we should, it seems to cover all the aspects that God would want us to be aware of. It could be used at Christmas or any other time – a way of getting our priorities right when we often stumble uneasily into meditation and prayer.

Lord Soper

Music, more than anything else, conjures up for me the beauty and meaning of Christmas. If I had to choose one piece of music more than any other, it would be the tune set to the Christmas hymn "Once in Royal David's City", which I hear every year in the carol service from King's College, Cambridge. As I hear the piping voice of the chorister beginning that Christmas hymn in the echoing silence of that great chapel, I am transported into the world of wonder and truth and goodness that Christmas means for me; and I am ever grateful for that recurring experience.

Once in royal David's city
Stood a lowly cattle shed,
Where a mother laid her baby
In a manger for his bed;
Mary was that mother mild,
Jesus Christ her little child.

He came down to earth from heaven
Who is God and Lord of all,
And his shelter was a stable,
And his cradle was a stall;
With the poor, and mean, and lowly,
Lived on earth our Saviour holy.

And, through all his wondrous childhood,
He would honour and obey,
Love, and watch the lowly maiden,
In whose gentle arms he lay;

Christian children all must be
Mild, obedient, good as he.

For he is our childhood's pattern,
Day by day like us he grew,
He was little, weak, and helpless,
Tears and smiles like us he knew;
And he feeleth for our sadness,
And he shareth in our gladness.

And our eyes at last shall see him,
Through his own redeeming love,
For that child so dear and gentle
Is our Lord in heaven above;
And he leads his children on
To the place where he is gone.

Not in that poor lowly stable,
With the oxen standing by,
We shall see him; but in heaven,
Set at God's right hand on high;
When like stars his children crowned
All in white shall wait around.

Delia Smith

Christmas Eve (evening). Sometimes, at this time on Christmas Eve, I find myself recalling some lines from Shakespeare – the scene on the battlements at Elsinore:

> Some say, that ever 'gainst that season comes
> Wherein our Saviour's birth is celebrated,
> The bird of dawning singeth all night long;
> And then, they say, no spirit can walk abroad;
> The nights are wholesome; then no planets strike,
> No fairy takes, nor witch hath power to charm,
> So hallow'd and so gracious is the time.
>
> (Hamlet I.i.158–164)

For me it captures the magic tranquillity of the moment, the peacefulness. I only recently discovered that, historically, at the time of Christ's birth, the world (that is to say, the Roman world) *was* at peace. The earlier civil wars had been resolved, and the frontiers, including Judaea, were settled for a time. The gates of the temple of Mars in the Forum at Rome were closed, apparently for the first and last time. "How silently, how silently, the wondrous gift is given." The Prince of Peace born in an interlude when there was peace on earth.

To experience the wonder of this holy night we need to take time to be silent and alone. I still remember, as a small child, on Christmas Eve when everyone else seemed preoccupied, stealing away to the room where the Christmas tree was. I would turn out the room lights and just sit staring at the tree shimmering and sparkling with jewelled lights, letting my eyes feast on the beauty of it all. With the passing years the initial wonder of the Christmas tree has faded a little perhaps, but the marvel of faith has increased, and I still feel the need to go somewhere quiet and silently feast on the wonder of this holy night. Sometimes it might be outside in the frosty night, just gazing at the (hopefully clear and starry) sky, pondering the mystery of what took place in Bethlehem two thousand years ago. The thoughts are always the same: How can it be? How could almighty God actually become man – one of us? Yet we dare to believe it. This is our faith. This is the divine exchange, Jesus humbling himself to share in our humanity in order that we may share his divinity. We can only confess with the psalmist that "such knowledge is beyond my understanding, a height to which my mind cannot attain" (139 [138]:6).

Christmas Eve (midnight). When Mary brought forth her son there was no royal fanfare, no twenty-one-gun salute, no balcony announcement to the waiting throng, no flash-bulbs, TV cameramen or teleprinter messages. Outside the stable the crowds in Bethlehem went about their business, unaware that anything momentous was happening other than the census that had brought them there in the first place. But heaven was celebrating the birthday of life, life for all mankind. "And suddenly with the angel there was a great throng of the heavenly host, praising God and singing: 'Glory to God in the highest . . . and peace to men' " (Luke 2:13–14).

Significantly the only ones to whom this was communicated were the shepherds, quiet in the fields outside the village. Modern theologians may make light of the shepherds, but for me they symbolize the poor in spirit, those humble enough to seek and find God in our mundane human circumstances: they gazed into the clear and starry night and *saw* the light. We should, like the shepherds, be humble enough to seek the Christ child and kneel before the manger with nothing to offer but the poverty of being human. Our lives we *can* offer; we can pray, Come and rescue me and redeem the whole of my life so that I may join the heavenly throng and see the vision of your glory. Join the angels and cry: "Glory to God in the highest, and peace to all men."

Christmas in Prison

RICHARD WURMBRAND

*Richard Wurmbrand, a Romanian pastor, was held in
Communist jails for fourteen years. Accused of being part
of an imperialist spy network, his only crime was to
preach about Jesus Christ. In spite of undergoing torture,
solitary confinement, and spending several years in the
"death room" which no man had ever left alive, he not
only survived but brought many fellow prisoners to faith
in Christ before his release in 1964. Here he describes one
Christmas in prison.*

Winter came on, with heavy snowstorms. Thick icicles hung
from the roof, and hoar frost patterned the window-panes.
Outside the cold made you gasp. By December the snow was
six feet deep. It was the coldest winter for a hundred years,
so they said. There was no heating, but until now we had two
or three blankets each, instead of the regulation one, for
every time a man died in Room Four we took his bedclothes.
Then there was a check – and we were left with a single
covering each. We slept in our clothes all winter. Often we
were without bread. The soup, made of carrots too rotten to
be sold, became still thinner.

On Christmas Eve, prison talk became more serious.
There were few quarrels, no swearing, little laughter. Every
man thought of those he loved and there was a feeling of
communion with the rest of mankind, which was usually so
remote from our lives.

I spoke of Christ, but all the time my feet and hands were
cold as steel, my teeth chattered, and an icy lump of hunger
in my stomach seemed to spread through my body until only
the heart lived. When I stopped, a simple farming lad took up

where I had left off. Aristar had never been to school. Yet he talked so naturally, describing the scene of the nativity as if it had happened in his own barn that week, that there were tears in the eyes of all who listened.

Someone began to sing in the prison that evening. At first his voice was quiet, and hardly came in among the thoughts that occupied my mind, of my wife and my son. But gradually the voice swelled wonderfully in the crisp, clear air until it echoed through the corridors and everybody stopped what they were doing.

We were very quiet when he ceased. The guards, huddled in their quarters around a coke stove, did not stir all evening. We began to tell stories, and when I was asked for one, I thought of the song, and told them this old Jewish legend:

King Saul of Israel brought David, the shepherd honoured for killing Goliath, to his court. David loved music, and he was delighted to see a harp of great beauty standing in the palace. Saul said, "I paid much for that instrument, but I was deceived. It gives forth only ugly sounds."

David took it up to try, and drew from it music so exquisite that every man was moved. The harp seemed to laugh and sing and weep. King Saul asked, "How is it that all the musicians I called brought discord from this harp, and only you could bring out music?"

David, the future king, replied, "Before me, each man tried to play his own song on these strings. But I sang to the harp its own song. I recalled how it had been a young tree, with birds that chirped in its branches and limbs green with leaves that blossomed in the sun. I reminded it of the day when men came to cut it down; and you heard it weep under my fingers. I explained then that this is not the end. Its death as a tree meant the start of a new life in which it would glorify God, as a harp; and you heard how it rejoiced under my hands.

"So when the Messiah comes, many will try to sing on his harp their own songs, and their tunes will be harsh. We must sing on his harp his own song, the song of his life, passions, joys, sufferings, death and resurrection. Only then will the music be true."

It was a song like this we heard that Christmas in the jail of Tirgul-Ocna.

The Ending of the Year

When trees did show no leaves,
    And grass no daisies had,
And fields had lost their sheaves,
    And streams in ice were clad,
And day of light was shorn,
    And wind had got a spear,
Jesus Christ was born
    In the ending of the year.

Like green leaves when they grow,
    He shall for comfort be;
Like life in streams shall flow,
    For running water he;
He shall raise hope like corn
    For barren fields to bear,
And therefore he was born
    In the ending of the year.

Like daisies to the grass,
    His innocence he'll bring;
In keenest winds that pass
    His flowering love shall spring;
The rising of the morn
    At midnight shall appear,
Whenever Christ is born
    In the ending of the year.

                                    Eleanor Farjeon

Crisis at Christmas

LORD MURRAY OF EPPING FOREST

No, not the sort of crisis that the splendid charity which is benefiting from the royalties of this book copes with at Christmastime – and throughout the year. This involved a very un-Christmassy party at which the reluctant guests were the unions from the Rubery Owen factory near Wolverhampton.

For some time the Amalgamated Engineering Union and the Electrical Engineering Union had been accusing the Transport and General Workers' Union of trying to poach their members, and the animosity between the "brothers" had reached the point where there was a real danger of the factory stopping work – and with it a good part of the West Midlands motor industry for which it made essential parts.

Just before Christmas the management told the unions that, if they couldn't sort out their problems and work normally, the factory would close on 1st January. Some managements make that sort of threat more often than they have cold dinners, but when I heard about it on Christmas Eve I was convinced they meant it. So I decided the TUC must get involved, and quickly.

It was too late to call the unions in for talks that day. When I started ringing round I proposed a meeting the next day – Christmas Day – not because I believed for a moment we would get it, but to concentrate their minds and make them feel that leaving it to Boxing Day would be a real concession to their families.

With a bit of pushing, Moss Evans of the TGWU, helpful as always, agreed to come to Congress House with his local representatives at 3 p.m. on Boxing Day. One up, two to go.

Hughie Scanlon of the AEU, after offering me – courteously – his views on the TGWU and on my own sanity, agreed to come, provided he could be away by six o'clock. "No problem, Hughie", I said, noting mentally that he hadn't said 6 p.m., and that he might possibly have meant 6 a.m. Two up.

I had deliberately left Frank Chapple of the ETU until last, and I didn't reach him until nearly ten o'clock. After I had explained my proposal to him there was a long silence. It might be Christmas Eve, but I didn't think Frank was saying his prayers (though I was). I repeated my request. His reply was – as usual – cheerful but unprintable. "Frank," I said, "what about a bit of goodwill to all men? And don't forget that it's your members who get laid off next week. And I'm going ahead with the meeting anyhow now that the others have agreed to come." Reason (or something) prevailed, at least to the point where Frank agreed that his President should come. By this time I knew that I could eat my Christmas dinner in peace. The fact that they had, with a bit of prodding, agreed to come to a meeting on Boxing Day meant that they were seriously looking for an answer to the problem.

So it turned out at that memorable Boxing Day meeting. Oh, it still had its ups and downs. No, Hughie didn't get back to his wife by 6 p.m; around that time I recall standing holding the doorhandle and asking for just another half-hour. And I well remember the explosion that blew up after we had put together an agreement which settled the issue and provided for the unions' full-time officials to visit the factory the following week to dot the i's. Duggie, the chief TGWU shop steward in the factory – a real Staffordshire bull-terrier he was – told his General Secretary that no full-time official would go into the factory without Duggie's permission, which he had no intention of giving. What Moss Evans said (or did) to Duggie in the corridor I never knew – I never asked – but it worked.

I would like to think that Christmas – the time above all for reconciliation – helped to concentrate everybody's mind that little bit harder on resolving their joint problem.

Christmas Eve
Carols in a Hospice
(Based on the talk given to the
Hospice choir, Christmas 1985)

DAME CICELY SAUNDERS

On Christmas Eve a choir of some seventy people of all ages
comes together for a brief rehearsal and a cheering drink and
then sets out to sing two carols in each of the four wards of St
Christopher's Hospice. In each ward we then walk in proces-
sion, led by the latest Hospice baby in its mother's arms,
humming our last carol, and so up to the next ward. The
Hospice windows are outlined by candles for this one hour
and for a short time afterwards, when all the singers and staff
rush out and see the bay windows of the Hospice lit up and a
bright star of David on the roof.

Each year we meet for this short rehearsal and set out, a
motley crew of staff, volunteers and their families, to sing
round the darkened wards, lit only by the candles that line the
windows. We come to represent the whole Hospice family
and to greet those who are here tonight, the patients and the
families and nurses who sit with them.

Some beds are empty. A few people have become well
enough to be discharged, others have gone for a few days at
home, and beds are also empty because someone has come
to the end of their journey. We keep them so for a day or two
while the family comes back and we all remember them.

We are led this year by Laura, our youngest-ever carol
baby, only two weeks old but held safely in the arms of her
proud mother, recently one of our staff nurses. She is a

perfect symbol to illustrate our singing. It is very important on a Hospice Christmas Eve to sing of God's sharing in all our dependence and vulnerability, for he showed this in such a way as to transform and fully make new and heal all wounds.

Every word of each carol matters to those who listen, but we are also singing for each other, with more or less talent, because we wanted to share together in this one evening. But we are not singing only to those waiting up in the wards, still less only to each other. We are celebrating and singing to love – the love that welcomes everyone who has love to offer – the love of the power that created the farthest galaxies come down in an unbelievably fine focus to the incarnation of a lowly birth in one point of time and space. That was truly a place humble enough for our Christmas offerings in this Hospice, our home-made crib and the manger in the chapel, our candles set simply in jam jars and our one-off carols. We are singing to love: love as given to us in our daily life through the love of others, but given supremely in the life of Jesus, given to us as on this night.

Some of us see this sharply and clearly, others only dimly and with many hesitations, but we all know we can never fully grasp the unimaginable love God has for us. We can only rejoice that we can reach out together in trust, believing that as we sing as best we can it may help those upstairs to join with us in finding those incredible words fresh once again in all the truth of poetry.

We will finish here, after humming our way back through the Hospice, with our final carol "Hark the Herald Angels Sing". We surely do not have the voices of angels but the glory we celebrate is the same because it is his, and for him no gift is too humble for notice and for acceptance.

Let us now give our singing to him and to all upstairs in the four wards – knowing that he gives himself to us.

Hark, the herald-angels sing
"Glory to the new-born King,
Peace on earth and mercy mild,
God and sinners reconciled!"
Joyful, all ye nations, rise,
Join the triumph of the skies;
With the angelic host proclaim,
"Christ is born in Bethlehem".
  Hark the herald angels sing,
  "Glory to the new-born King".

Christ, by highest heaven adored,
Christ, the everlasting Lord,
Late in time behold him come,
Offspring of a virgin's womb,
Veiled in flesh the Godhead see;
Hail, the incarnate Deity,
Pleased as Man with man to dwell,
Jesus, our Immanuel!

Hail, the heaven-born Prince of Peace!
Hail, the Son of Righteousness!
Light and life to all he brings,
Risen with healing in his wings.
Mild he lays his glory by,
Born that man no more may die,
Born to raise the sons of earth,
Born to give them second birth:
  Hark the herald angels sing,
  "Glory to the new-born king".

Baroness Masham of Ilton

When I was a child I lived in the very north of Scotland. One Christmas during the Second World War provided a lasting memory that remains with me to this day.

Many Polish service personnel came to Caithness during the war, and that Christmas some of the officers, from a cavalry regiment, came and had Christmas dinner with us. Afterwards, in the light of the candles on the Christmas tree, they sang Polish carols. As they stood on the staircase with the tree towering upwards from the hall, I noticed tears pouring down the cheeks of these grown men. The love of their faraway country and the special unity of Christmas makes me always remember that Christmas is special. It is the celebration of Christ's Mass.

I have noticed that Christmas is special for people in prison, too. Young prisoners with whom I have worked feel more homesick then than at any other time. Christmas is a time for unity and that is why so many people feel a crisis when they are far from home and lonely. If they will think of the unity of Christ, perhaps that loneliness will be eased.

A Village Christmas

ANN PARKINSON

Living in a small village like Northaw and being in the church choir is one way of being part of a small community. This never more so than at Christmas. Our parish is large and the

Vicar has two churches in it, so Christmas is particularly busy for him.

For many years now we have invited four families, all close friends, to join us on Christmas Eve. All the children are now grown up, but they are encouraged to bring friends along as well, so the numbers vary. The pleasure never alters, and we all enjoy seeing each other again, catching up on news and renewing friendships. After a very simple meal, we choose two captains for two teams. We then play silly games and charades. The main aim of the latter is to catch out the oldies with hideously difficult names of books, plays and films. The acting gets better each year, and the evening passes quickly. Then the church bells ring, and we all troop to Midnight Mass. The church looks beautiful, lit by hundreds of candles flickering in the draughts, while the singing thunders to the high roof. Our little choir makes no impact, but helps in leading the responses in the Communion service. Afterwards it is hot chocolate and coffee for us all and then home and to bed. A good start to a Christmas Day.

Later that morning I am back in church for the service of nine lessons and carols. This is a lovely family service, and the church echoes with noise of babies and young children. Those who read a lesson range in age from our youngest choir member of about eleven to our much-loved patron, Major Dore, who is well into his nineties.

The nine lessons we read and the carols we sing never change. The message, the story of Christ's birth, is the same, and yet it always seems to strike a different note for me. So often in the weeks before, buying presents and food, sending cards and organizing the four days around Christmas, I feel it is all too much. How often I hear and echo other people's moans about the pressures of Christmas – so little of its joy and real meaning remains.

And so in the church a sense of peace and contentment returns. The repeated message of Christ's love for us all encourages me to remember the joy, pain and joy again of his birth, death and resurrection. In the months that follow, this special Christmas story helps me when problems and difficulties inevitably arise.

So Christmas, through the intertwining of church, family and friends, brings a renewal of hope and sustains me for the months ahead until I repeat it all the next year.

Bells Ringing

I heard bells ringing
Suddenly all together, one wild, intricate figure,
A mixture of wonder and praise
Climbing the winter-winged air in December.
Norwich, Gloucester, Salisbury, combined with York
To shake Worcester and Paul's into the old discovery
Made frost-fresh again.
I heard these rocketing and wound-remembering chimes
Running their blessed counterpoint
Round the mazes of my mind,
And felt their message brimming over with love,
Watering my cold heart,
Until, as over all England hundreds of towers trembled
Beneath the force of Christmas rolling out,
I knew, as shepherds and magi knew,
That all sounds had been turned into one sound,
And a single golden bell,
Repeating, as knees bowed, the name EMMANUEL.

Leonard Clark

The Bishop of Peterborough

Most of us like to write of our successes. It is natural and harmless. However, here is the story of a Christmas failure.

Many years ago when I was Vicar of St Peter Mancroft, Norwich, our Christmases were splendid and our services were attended by a lot of people. On Christmas morning, after the grandeur of the Festival of Nine Lessons and Carols and Midnight Eucharist, we had a simple carol-strewn family service. At this I preached a sermon on "Let Us Now Go to Bethlehem", suggesting that the shepherds may well have been East Anglians, as that ancient construction of the English which puts "now" before the verb was then common usage in Norfolk and Suffolk. I went on to talk about how we delay, and urged the congregation to "do it now", to respond immediately to the impulse for good as it struck them.

At the end of the service a charming young woman whom I knew slightly came and said to me that her family was divided about church attendance. Her husband really did disapprove of it and she felt that her marriage was to some degree threatened by this division. She had decided she must give way, for she loved him. In view of my sermon she intended to do it now and would not be coming to church again . . .

Not my most successful sermon, and yet one listener did what I had suggested.

Group Captain Leonard Cheshire

Christmas 1948 is the one that stands out above all others in my memory. It was the Christmas that I was received into the Church, and the first Christmas at Le Court, where my work amongst disabled people began. We were living more or less from hand to mouth, not really knowing where the money could come from to pay the weekly bills. There were twelve heavily disabled people in the house, some of them old and approaching the end of their life, and only one resident full-time helper other than myself. From one source or another we had managed to find a small present for everyone, but it looked as if there would be nothing special for Christmas dinner, until at the last moment, and completely out of the blue, a hamper arrived from Canada. It came from the Canadian ex-members of the Dambusters who – I don't know how – had heard something about Le Court and wanted to say Happy Christmas.

The combination of this, of having been received into the Church earlier in the day, and of preparing myself for my first Midnight Mass, gave me a sense of wonder that I had never before felt. Everything that evening seemed "with grace divine imbued", especially the stars. The stars so distant and yet in another sense so close and so friendly, deepened yet further my feeling of wonder that the Creator himself, who lives in light inaccessible, should come amongst us in the form of a baby, born in a manger in Bethlehem.

Infant holy, infant lowly,
for his bed a cattle stall;
Oxen lowing, little knowing
Christ the babe is Lord of all.
Swift are winging angels singing,
Nowells ringing, tidings bringing,
Christ the babe is Lord of all,
Christ the babe is Lord of all.

Flocks were sleeping, shepherds keeping
Vigil till the morning new,
Saw the glory, heard the story,
Tidings of a gospel true.
Thus rejoicing, free from sorrow,
Praises voicing, greet the morrow,
Christ the babe was born for you,
Christ the babe was born for you.

E.M.G. Reed

Christmas in Belfast

NICK PAGE

Spending Christmas with the Army in Belfast was a novel and rich experience. Before flying into Aldergrove the TV images went through my mind: bombs exploding and bullets flying. I expected an almost tangible atmosphere of fear and hate. How wrong I was.

I went to Northern Ireland to present, for BBC Radio Two, a programme of records and conversations with guests, live from Holywood Barracks – temporary home of the 3rd Battalion of the Royal Regiment of Fusiliers. It is always said that Christmas is a family festival, which is perhaps why the regiment entered into it so enthusiastically. From the Colonel down I heard the same thing: "This is more than a regiment, it's a family."

In spite of the regiment's serious and dangerous work, the barracks had seen a plethora of celebrations and parties in the days leading up to the 25th; the men, with their wives and families, marking Christmas like any community anywhere. For those without wives and children on station a special camaraderie is supported by a number of traditions. Each man is woken by an officer bearing an offering of "gunfire" – a concoction which originates not from the arsenal but the cookhouse. This potent brew is tea laced with something rather stronger!

The "last shall be first" style of service also operated for the Christmas lunch. We sat down with the men to a traditional spread of turkey with all the trimmings, served to us by the officers – as to the manner born. The only item of uniform that was compulsory here was the paper hat. While eating we were serenaded with a selection of seasonal music by the battalion band. The bandmaster, who was also a member of the Salvation Army, told me that to him Christmas was not only great fun, but that it also meant "God's gift to me of Jesus Christ".

During the morning we visited the barracks chapel. Single men and families joined together (those that were of a mind to do so) in the special family service led by the Chaplain. The children featured strongly in the retelling of the Christmas story round the crib -- even if one boy did upstage Mary and Joseph by sticking a shepherd between them! Wives and girlfriends joined with the men in a choir formed to provide the Christmas music.

We could almost have been in any church worshipping Jesus Christ and celebrating his birthday – except for the arrival of the Colonel and the Regimental Sergeant Major. They appeared not only in uniform but with muddy boots as they had been out since early morning, visiting the troops on patrol on the streets of the city – a reminder of what purpose lay behind this community.

Christmas in Belfast points up the contrasts in the life of the city. I remember standing outside the City Hall listening to a choir of schoolgirls gathered round a crib singing "Mary's Boy Child". All around were the traditional decorations, the words Peace and Joy appearing frequently. Yet over the road was a checkpoint – a massive steel barricade manned by armed police and soldiers. Many of those passing through (simply to get to Woolworths or Marks & Spencer) were being searched for guns or bombs.

I asked one of the company commanders how, as a Christian, he coped with the tension of following Jesus and living in the violence and hate around him. He said that most people were "peace-lovers", but that some people were also called to be "peace-makers". "I like to think I'm a peace-lover and also a peace-maker."

Our human attempts to bring peace between men may meet with varying degrees of success. However, Jesus was born to bring us peace with God. He came into a world of violence and hate, of great privilege and untold suffering. A world, in fact, which rejected him and had turned its back on God. A world just like ours. He came to offer us a dimension of life which has the potential to overcome hate with love, to replace violence with peace. That dimension of life is his life in us. That is the heart of our celebration of Christmas – in Belfast or anywhere else.

Viscount Tonypandy

My heart glows at the thought of Christmas. Friends whom I have not talked to for a long time send me greetings, and I do the same for them.

We have good cause for sending greetings to each other at Christmas, because it is a reminder of the best news that ever came to the world. The fact that God sent his only Son into the world to live among us is still exciting news. It is because of Christ's coming to the world that we know what God is like, and how his Holy Spirit is always with us. I therefore love the Christmas carols and all the celebrations.

Older people like myself find Christmas in a different way from that of children. For the young the thrill is wrapped up in the parties and in the giving and receiving of presents.

Memories of other Christmases are part of life for older people. The first Christmas after my dear mother died, I thought to myself: "I can't bear to be home: I will go abroad." It was an emotional decision which in fact was foolish. As soon as my plane landed in the Middle East, I said to myself: "George, you are being silly: wherever you go your memories go with you." No one can escape the reality of memories that can tear at the heartstrings, but I thank God that no one can travel so far that he or she is out of the presence of God's comforting Holy Spirit.

At Christmas now, I rejoice in my memories and thank God for them. I also thank God that Christmas is a reminder that he cares for me. God *never* forgets us – that's what Christmas means.

4

See Amid the Winter Snow

The Challenge of Christmas

✠

Jesus was born in the town of Bethlehem in Judaea, during the time when Herod was king. Soon afterwards, some men who studied the stars came from the east to Jerusalem and asked, "Where is the baby born to be the king of the Jews? We saw his star when it came up in the east, and we have come to worship him."

When King Herod heard about this, he was very upset, and so was everyone else in Jerusalem. He called together all the chief priests and the teachers of the Law and asked them, "Where will the Messiah be born?"

"In the town of Bethlehem in Judaea", they answered. "For this is what the prophet wrote:

> 'Bethlehem in the land of Judah,
> you are by no means the least of the
> leading cities of Judah;
> for from you will come a leader
> who will guide my people Israel.' "

So Herod called the visitors from the east to a secret meeting and found out from them the exact time the star had appeared. Then he sent them to Bethlehem with these instructions: "Go and make a careful search for the child, and when you find him, let me know, so that I too may go and worship him."

And so they left, and on their way they saw the same star they had seen in the east. When they saw it, how happy they were, what joy was theirs! It went ahead of them until it stopped over the place where the child was. They went into the house, and when they saw the child with his mother

Mary, they knelt down and worshipped him. They brought out their gifts of gold, frankincense, and myrrh, and presented them to him.

Then they returned to their country by another road, since God had warned them in a dream not to go back to Herod (Matthew 2:1–12).

Christmas Is Really
For The Children

Christmas is really
for the children.
Especially for children
who like animals, stables,
stars and babies wrapped
in swaddling clothes.
Then there are wise men,
kings in fine robes,
humble shepherds and a
hint of rich perfume.

Easter is not really
for the children
unless accompanied by
a cream-filled egg.
It has whips, blood, nails,
a spear and allegations
of body snatching.
It involves politics, God
and the sins of the world.
It is not good for people
of a nervous disposition.
They would do better to
think of rabbits, chickens
and the first snowdrop
of spring.

Or they'd do better to
wait for a re-run of
Christmas without asking
too many questions about
what Jesus did when he grew up
or whether there's any connection.

Steve Turner

But Suppose It's True . . .

CLIFF RICHARD

Which kind of Christmas is yours?

The one you have to struggle into, maybe like an old suit, somewhere early in December? The one that demands you make an effort to be friendly, find time to send cards to people who might send them to you, and generally spend more money than normal to create the right impression? Inside there is the gnawing awareness that, come Twelfth Night when the cards and the Christmas tree are ditched, the play-acting will end and the real world will lurch back into focus. It's the motiveless Christmas. We send greetings, give presents, eat, drink and try to be merry because society says we should. It's December and that's how people in the West are expected to behave at that time of year. The result is often destructive – a lot of people become acutely lonely, depressed and envious. The family next door is having a great time, so we reckon, but our circumstances are different.

If only contentment and fun could be switched on that easily. Of course they can't.

But there's the other Christmas – the real one, the one with the motive, the one that has Jesus in focus. I know you can't switch that on either. You can't make yourself believe him or love him – but can you understand that he makes sense of it all – the cards and the gifts, the parties and the daft hats? Just suppose for a moment that it really is true – that God really did love the world so much that he gave . . . It would revolutionize your Christmas – not to mention the rest of the year!

Someone once asked a Christian friend of mine, "Supposing you're wrong about Christianity?" My friend replied, "If I'm wrong, I'll have lost nothing and still had a fabulous life. But suppose you're wrong . . ?"

A Christmas Present

GERALD PRIESTLAND

I think this is the right time to examine the theory and practice – the theology, even – of Christmas presents. I read that it goes back to the Roman Saturnalia, though the Church had endeavoured to paint this out by superimposing the example of the Magi, with their gifts of gold and myrrh and frankincense. This, however, takes us well into the New Year – to the Epiphany – and the fact is that until fairly recently, gifts were a New Year phenomenon, with servants receiving new clothes and the poor a handout to help them through the worst of the winter still to come.

Doting upon children at Christmas time is, again, a relatively late arrival. True, they had their day on the Feast of the Holy Innocents or "Childermass" (which is 28th December), or on St Nicholas' Day (which is 6th December), and sometimes this included the election of a boy bishop. But the giving of presents to children as members of the family does not seem to have caught on at Christmas proper until the early eighteenth century. It may have been prompted by the pestering of servants and tradespeople for their "Christmas boxes". Certainly it isn't until then that we find specially designed Christmas gifts being advertised; and the custom of exchanging presents round the tree seems to have been introduced to England from Germany by Prince Albert, in about 1841.

A newspaper once advertised: "FOR SALE: Unwanted present – make ideal gift", and I must say my heart sinks when I encounter a Gift Shop. The Gift is almost by definition something you would want so little yourself that there's no sacrifice involved in giving it away. Which is surely all wrong.

Or is it? The present Cousin Roger would like is not necessarily a favourite of *yours*. Thoughtfulness is obviously part of good giving; but it isn't particularly thoughtful to give everyone what you would have liked. Do I come down to giving them all book or record tokens? – at least a bit more thoughtful than cash, although I think it was Bernard Shaw who said that the advantage of getting money was that it enabled you to have what you wanted, rather than what other people thought you ought to have.

But should we be giving presents at all? Once they're into their forties, most people have everything they really need; so isn't the rest extravagance? Shouldn't we be sending money to charity? There are so many people in need all over the world, and the great charitable organizations make it so easy for us to help them. Hasn't Christmas become almost totally secularized? Shouldn't we just go to church and ignore the rest of it?

I think that would be a pity. I can't remember that Jesus gave or received many presents; but he was a notorious party-goer, and by no means a kill-joy. People complained about his lack of asceticism. So I don't think we should feel guilty about having fun or giving pleasure. And it is a pleasure to give or receive a well-chosen gift. Yes, of course we should remember the charities: I think it's all the better when a family, school or office bands together to make a collection. And it may well be that we can save the money by scaling our Christmas presents down from their sometimes ridiculous heights. Christmas ought to be a time of family reunion and mutual caring, and presents (seen in that light) can be full of meaning.

May I offer – too late, perhaps – a few hints. Start planning your presents well ahead; keep a page in your diary to jot down ideas. Presents you see this Christmas may give you ideas for next. And, as a potential receiver, it can be positively helpful to others if you start dropping quiet hints some time in November: "Ah, I wish I had the new edition

. . . I wonder if there's a recording of that . . . My secateurs are falling apart."

But none of this will affect those whom I regard as (morally) the best givers: they have already planted their bowls of bulbs, potted their jams and pickles, knitted their socks and gloves. Mind you – it's sometimes an effort to say "Thank you" with enthusiasm; but if God loves a cheerful giver, he's a right to expect a cheerful receiver, too.

Fiona Castle

As Christmas approaches I become so swept up in the commercial aspect of it that it's hard to retain the real meaning of it all.

This is the dilemma in which many Christians find themselves. How many Christmas cards? What to buy for whom? How many to dinner? Which parties to go to? New clothes? More decorations? It seems that Jesus is pushed into a corner and sometimes neglected altogether. As a Christian, I am also torn by my plenty compared with the poverty of the Third World.

One day I poured my feelings out to God. I didn't know what to do. I knew I was spending more than I should and giving our children more than they needed. But I didn't want them to be deprived just because of my conscience – and after all, their friends were also being over-indulged.

I had such a lovely reassurance from the Lord at this time that I felt it was worth sharing it with others facing the same agonies of conscience and heart-searching. I sensed that God was telling me that he understood what I was going through. He knew I was torn between present-giving and channelling my giving towards those who are really needy. He showed me that if I bought my presents for each person lovingly, thoughtfully and carefully, and wrapped them with similar attention, God would be pleased. If I made decorations with the family to make them happy, then it would also please Jesus. If I prepared food for each occasion with love in my heart for each person who would be enjoying it, then God would receive my love too. In fact, if I did all my work "as unto the Lord", it would please him.

So as Christmas approaches, relax and allow God to guide

you in all the preparations for the festivities. You will find 𝑡
however much tinsel surrounds your Christmas, Christ will
still be the centre of everything you do.

African Christmas

Here are no signs of festival,
No holly and no mistletoe,
No robin and no crackling fire,
And no soft, feathery fall of snow.

In England one could read the words
Telling how shepherds in the fold
Followed the star and reached the barn
Which kept the Saviour from the cold.

And picture in one's mind the scene –
The tipsy, cheerful foreign troops,
The kindly villagers who stood
About the child in awkward groups.

But in this blazing Christmas heat
The ox, the ass, the bed of hay,
The shepherds and the Holy Child
Are stilted figures in a play.

Exiles, we see that we, like slaves,
To symbol and to memory,
Have worshipped, not the incarnate Christ,
But tinsel on the Christmas tree.

John Press

Where Is the Child?

LUIS PALAU

Many years ago a wealthy European family decided to have their newborn baby baptized in their enormous mansion. Dozens of guests were invited to the elaborate affair, and they all arrived dressed in the latest fashions. After depositing their elegant wraps on a bed in an upstairs room, the guests were entertained royally. Soon the time came for the main purpose of their gathering, the infant's baptismal ceremony. But where was the child? No one seemed to know.

The children's governess ran upstairs, only to return with a desperate look on her face. Everyone began searching frantically for the baby. Someone recalled having seen the child sleeping on one of the beds. The baby was on a bed, all right – buried underneath a pile of coats, jackets and furs. The very object of that day's celebration had been forgotten, neglected, and nearly destroyed!

I can't help but remember that story as I walk along busy city streets during this holiday season. Everywhere I look, I see lights, tinsel, trimmings and trappings. Shoppers loaded down with expensive gifts they will spend the next year paying off. And I ask myself, "Is this Christmas?" Where is the Child whose birthday we celebrate?

I'm all for celebrating Christmas. But the Christmas you and I so often see is one of commercialism and excesses. The true Christmas demonstrates God's love for the world, as the Bible says in 1 John 4:9–10. "This is how God showed his love among us: he sent his one and only Son into the world that we might live through him. This is love: not that we loved God, but that he loved us and sent his Son as the atoning sacrifice for our sins."

Jesus Christ was God's love gift to the world. The Christ

Child of that first Christmas Day became a man who sacrificially died for the sins of the world and who rose again by the power of God. That is why, as we read in Romans 6:23, "the gift of God is eternal life in Christ Jesus our Lord."

Your Christmas, this year, can be the most meaningful holiday you have ever known. By receiving God's offer of eternal life in Christ, you can experience peace with God and peace in your heart. That's cause for celebration!

Where is the Child in *your* Christmas?

Bruce Kent

One of my very favourite pieces of Christmas reading is the Archbishop's moving Christmas sermon in T.S. Eliot's *Murder in the Cathedral*. By comparing the joy of Christmas Day with the memory of the stoning to death of St Stephen which we remember on 26th December every year, Eliot has given a real meaning to peace and Christmas.

The harsh part is that if we take our Christmas seriously as well as joyfully, we will inevitably be at cross purposes with the Caesar of the day. The result may not usually be martyrdom, but a Christianity which does not bring on its own troubles is not the Christianity we started out with.

"Glory to God in the highest, and on earth peace to men of good will." *The fourteenth verse of the second chapter of the Gospel according to Saint Luke*. In the Name of the Father, and of the Son, and of the Holy Ghost. Amen.

Dear children of God, my sermon this Christmas morning will be a very short one. I wish only that you should meditate in your hearts the deep meaning and mystery of our Masses of Christmas Day. For whenever Mass is said, we re-enact the Passion and Death of Our Lord; and on this Christmas Day we do this in celebration of his Birth. So that at the same moment we rejoice in his coming for the salvation of men, and offer again to God his Body and Blood in sacrifice, oblation and satisfaction for the sins of the whole world. It was in this same night that has just passed, that a multitude of the heavenly host appeared before the shepherds at Bethlehem, saying "Glory to God in the highest, and on earth peace to men of good will"; at this same time of all the year that we celebrate at once the Birth of Our Lord and his Passion and Death upon the Cross. Beloved, as the World sees, this is to behave in a strange fashion. For who in the World will both mourn and rejoice at once and for the same reason? For either joy will be overborne by mourning, or mourning will be cast out by joy; so it is only in these our Christian mysteries that we can rejoice and mourn at once for the same reason. Now think for a moment about the meaning of this word "peace". Does it seem strange to you that the angels should have announced Peace, when ceaselessly the world has been stricken with War and the fear of War? Does it seem to you that the angelic voices were mistaken, and that the promise was a disappointment and a cheat?

Reflect now, how Our Lord himself spoke of Peace. He said to his disciples, "Peace I leave with you, my peace I give unto you." Did he mean peace as we think of it: the kingdom of England at peace with its neighbours, the barons at peace with the King, the householder counting over his peaceful gains, the swept hearth, his best wine for a friend at the table, his wife singing to the children? Those men his disciples knew no such things: they went forth to journey afar, to suffer by land and sea, to know torture, imprisonment, disappointment, to suffer death by martyrdom. What

116

then did he mean? If you ask that, remember then that he said also, "Not as the world gives, give I unto you." So then, he gave to his disciples peace, but not peace as the world gives.

Consider also one thing of which you have probably never thought. Not only do we at the feast of Christmas celebrate at once Our Lord's Birth and his Death: but on the next day we celebrate the martyrdom of his first martyr, the blessed Stephen. Is it an accident, do you think, that the day of the first martyr follows immediately the day of the Birth of Christ? By no means. Just as we rejoice and mourn at once, in the Birth and in the Passion of Our Lord; so also, in a smaller figure, we both rejoice and mourn in the death of martyrs. We mourn, for the sins of the world that has martyred them; we rejoice, that another soul is numbered among the Saints in Heaven, for the glory of God and for the salvation of men.

Beloved, we do not think of a martyr simply as a good Christian who has been killed because he is a Christian: for that would be solely to mourn. We do not think of him simply as a good Christian who has been elevated to the company of the Saints: for that would be simply to rejoice: and neither our mourning nor our rejoicing is as the world's is. A Christian martyrdom is never an accident, for Saints are not made by accident. Still less is a Christian martyrdom the effect of a man's will to become a Saint, as a man by willing and contriving may become a ruler of men. A martyrdom is always the design of God, for his love of men, to warn them and to lead them, to bring them back to his ways. It is never the design of man; for the true martyr is he who has become the instrument of God, who has lost his will in the will of God, and who no longer desires anything for himself, not even the glory of being a martyr. So thus as on earth the Church mourns and rejoices at once, in a fashion that the world cannot understand; so in Heaven the Saints are most high, having made themselves most low, and are seen, not as we

117

see them, but in the light of the Godhead from which they draw their being.

I have spoken to you today, dear children of God, of the martyrs of the past, asking you to remember especially our martyr of Canterbury, the blessed Archbishop Elphege; because it is fitting, on Christ's birth day, to remember what is that Peace which he brought; and because, dear children, I do not think I shall ever preach to you again; and because it is possible that in a short time you may have yet another martyr, and that one perhaps not the last. I would have you keep in your hearts these words that I say, and think of them at another time. In the Name of the Father, and of the Son, and of the Holy Ghost. Amen.

See, amid the winter's snow,
Born for us on earth below,
See, the tender Lamb appears,
Promised from eternal years.
   Hail, thou ever-blessed morn!
   Hail, redemption's happy dawn!
   Sing through all Jerusalem:
   Christ is born in Bethlehem!

Lo, within a manger lies
He who built the starry skies,
He who, throned in height sublime,
Sits amid the cherubim.

Say, ye holy shepherds, say,
What your joyful news today;
Wherefore have ye left your sheep
On the lonely mountain steep?

"As we watched at dead of night,
Lo, we saw a wondrous light:
Angels, singing peace on earth,
Told us of the Saviour's birth."

Sacred Infant, all divine,
What a tender love was thine,
Thus to come from highest bliss
Down to such a world as this!

Teach, O teach us, holy Child,
By thy face so meek and mild,
Teach us to resemble thee
In thy sweet humility.

Christmas with
620 People Just Like Me

JOANNA WADE

Crisis at Christmas's "Open Christmas" fills a gap, for there are at least thirty thousand homeless in London alone and around three thousand sleeping rough at any one time. A disused church, drill hall, industrial unit, office block and bus garage have in turn over the last seventeen years been a temporary home for thousands of people without anywhere to go at Christmas.

If you go down Whitehall on Christmas morning, the homeless, who normally disappear into the bustle of London, suddenly seem caught in a spotlight as they alone are still to be seen. They alone have nowhere to go and no one to be with at a time when almost everyone else is, by hook or by crook, at home with others. When the tube stations, the day centres and the cheap cafes that help to disguise the isolation of homelessness are shut, Crisis tries to give those who stay with us a special time, just like everyone else.

Over eight hundred volunteers, from students to retired bank managers, provide all the care for the hundreds that come to Crisis every year. We do not take names and numbers, but we know that over Christmas 1986 our team of hairdressers performed eight hundred haircuts, and there were still many uncut heads in the building. We counted the plates on Christmas Day and found we had served six hundred and twenty Christmas dinners: turkey, gravy, stuffing, sprouts, pudding – the works.

Before we open, drivers who offer help go round schools collecting their Christmas decorations, and when the walls of our huge empty space are hung with tinsel and the lines are broken by Christmas trees, things begin to look more festive. Others collect food (we can use anything from lychees to baked beans, although the latter are more useful!), clothes and all the equipment needed. Much is donated and people are very generous.

In 1986 the London Association for the Blind offered us a disused factory at the ninth hour, so we had only about two weeks to bring in hundreds of mattresses to lay down on the floor at night, spray the equivalent of thirty thousand square feet of blankets with solution to halt possible infestation, sort the mountains of clothes into categories and sizes (we aim to achieve a precise fit, not expect the people who stay with us to make do; the dinner jackets, silk dressing gowns and the like are sifted out and sold in more appropriate places where the customers own wardrobes!), put down floor covering, build a kitchen in a portacabin, make a vegetable store in the former guide dogs' kennels, plumb in the mobile shower unit and sterilize the first aid room.

Somehow all the work always gets done in time and we open as planned on 23rd December. Once open, we try to have as few rules as possible. The only serious one is that we do not allow bottles on the premises. We provide as many services as we can to help people restore themselves physically, but the most important thing we can do is talk: talk and listen and provide appreciation and comfort, which is a rare commodity. We have done some good if we can help some of those who stay with us to realize that they deserve a sense of self-respect – that it is an admirable thing to survive sleeping outside in sub-zero temperatures and still have the energy to keep clean and to preserve a sense of humour.

Very quickly those who volunteer to help at the "Open" begin to wonder whether they are helping for the sake of the homeless or for the sake of themselves, because of the deep feeling of satisfaction that the Open gives and the sense one has of having found the meaning of Christmas. I have learnt so much since I first came to this home-from-home eleven years ago that I can no longer analyse my motives, but I know that I cannot imagine Christmas spent any other way. I always smile when someone who has just finished their first year says to me, "You know, they are just people, the same as you and me!" I hope that I have helped the same message to pass the other way, too.

Chad Varah

Even those who know G.K. Chesterton's poems well, and who regard his "Lepanto" as the finest ballad in the English language, do not seem to know his poem "The House of Christmas", and I have never seen it in a Christmas anthology. The last verse of it came to my mind as I searched my memory for something which linked Christmas with those who are homeless in our own day. Here it is:

> To an open house in the evening
> Home shall all men come,
> To an older place than Eden,
> To a taller town than Rome:
> To the end of the way of the wandering star,
> To the things that cannot be, and that are;
> To the place where He was homeless,
> And all men are at home.

G.K. Chesterton

A Christmas Wish

CORRIE TEN BOOM

"I came that they might have life, and might have it abundantly." (John 10:10)

What do I wish for you for Christmas? That you may have the joy the shepherds had (see Luke 2:15–20).

The shepherds told everyone what had happened. They knew so much more than the other people in Bethlehem. They had heard the angel's message which the Lord had made known to them; they had seen the newborn babe. They had met Mary and Joseph. What did they do? They told everyone! Do we know more than those for whom Christmas means "Jingle Bells" and Santa Claus or who only prepare for Christmas by getting cards off at the right time and presents wrapped? They are trying to do their yearly duty, for they have done this ritual every year, afraid of what others will think if they don't.

Christmas is not a duty! Jesus' coming was a free gift to all of us. The only thing we can do is to prepare ourselves for his coming.

Christmas is a remembrance of his coming as a little baby. Let us be ready for that feast so that we can prepare others too.

What a joy to know him, Jesus Christ, who was born in Bethlehem, died at the cross for our sins, was resurrected, and is with us always unto the end of the world.

Let us do what the shepherds did, and tell everyone who will listen.

Malcolm Muggeridge

Christ's birth brought hope and *agape* into the world. *Agape*, charity, had never before been known.

My favourite Christmas reading is the St John's epistle, which prepares us for the most stupendous event in human history – the Incarnation.

Dear friends, let us love one another, because love comes from God. Whoever loves is a child of God and knows God. Whoever does not love does not know God, for God is love. And God showed his love for us by sending his only Son into the world, so that we might have life through him. This is what love is: it is not that we have loved God, but that he loved us and sent his Son to be the means by which our sins are forgiven.

Dear friends, if this is how God loved us, then we should love one another. No one has ever seen God, but if we love one another, God lives in union with us, and his love is made perfect in us.

We are sure that we live in union with God and that he lives in union with us, because he has given us his Spirit. And we have seen and tell others that the Father sent his Son to be the Saviour of the world. (1 John 4:7–14)

Marilyn Baker

I enjoy the fun of Christmas, but I feel that today it has become cheapened and commercialized. To me it·means the celebration of God's love, which is so real and personal in my life.

When we think of Christmas, it is easy to remember only the sweet, weak baby in the manger. But that baby was Jesus Christ, the supreme Creator, through whom the world was made. Everyone is searching for peace, but real peace can only come when we trust in God through all life's ups and downs. He is Lord and all-powerful, yet, incredibly, he came to serve people like us. Even death could not destroy him.

It was with all these thoughts in mind that I wrote the song "God Came Among Us". I change all the time and yet he never changes, and through all my inner conflicts he gives me a joy that is so deep and lasting. At Christmastime I am amazed as I remember again that the God who made the universe really did come among us.

God Came Among Us

God came among us, he became a man,
Became a baby though through him the world began.
He came to earth to bring us peace, but where is that peace
    today?
It can be found by those who will let him direct their way.

He came to serve to show men how much he cared,
Their joys and sorrows he so willingly shared.

He came to earth to bring us joy, but where is that joy today?
It can be found by those who let him wash their guilt away.

Death tried to hold him but it could not succeed.
He rose again and now we can be freed.
He longs to give eternal life to all who will simply receive,
Yes, to all who will open their hearts and just believe.

The Event That Set Heaven Singing

BILLY GRAHAM

Christmas is not just a date on the calendar. It is the celebration of the event that set heaven to singing, an event that gave the stars of the night sky a new brilliance.

As we come to Christmas, we again read the words the prophet spoke eight hundred years before the birth of Christ: "The people that walked in darkness have seen a great light." In this passage the prophet had his first glimpse of Christmas. It is the promise of the coming of Christ and the light that was to dawn upon the world. It heralds the entrance of God into human history. It is heaven descending to earth. It is as though a trumpeter had taken his stand upon the turrets of time and announced to a despairing, hopeless and frustrated world the coming of the Prince of Peace.

No informed person today will deny that the human race walks in darkness. There are dilemmas and problems that seemingly have no answer. Many competent observers not usually given to pessimism despair of solving the problems of the world; they suspect that we are people who not only walk in darkness but walk in darkness to our doom.

For years people have been seeking to organize human life without God. They have tried to thrust him out of the universe. Many secular critics are using subtle forms of attack against evangelical Christianity throughout the world. Because these modern critics find it hard to believe in God, they have transferred their faith to man. They have invented in the past few years a creed which is the worship of humanity. "Glory to man in the highest" is their theme.

This worship of human nature has grown in popularity because it feeds on our own conceit. We have been told in the past few years, especially in some of our classrooms, that there is no sin, that the human race has a bit of selfishness which time will correct. It flatters the egotism in us; it seems to make redemption unnecessary; it empties the cross of its meaning. People will grow better, we are told.

However, the failure to solve the problems of the world in the past few years has shattered the hopes of many. We are more unsure of peace and have less freedom than ever before. We have built a world of television and spaceships, but we also have the possibility of radiation poisoning and mass suicide. In our brilliance without God we have become fools.

We look at the world today and wonder at the incredible folly of it – the ignorant conceit, the puffed-up egotism of the human race during the past few years. It is obvious that unredeemed man without the help of God will take the path of destruction, judgement and hell. We stand on the very edge of Armageddon.

The Hebrew propets such as Isaiah, Jeremiah and Ezekiel not only believed in God but they worshipped God. They believed that God could be seen in nature. They believed that he had made the world. But all through the centuries they seem to have been saying, "I wish that God would become personal."

This is precisely what he did that first Christmas night. He became personal in Bethlehem. "The Word was made flesh, and dwelt among us . . . No man hath seen God at any time; the only begotten Son, which is in the bosom of the Father, he hath declared him." At a specific time and at a specific place a specific Person was born and that Person was God of very God, the Lord Jesus Christ.

From the lips of Jesus came these words: "The Son of man is come to seek and to save that which was lost." Like piercing trumpets these words herald the breaking in of the Divine into human history. What a wonderful and glorious hope we have because of that first Christmas!

Christ came into a world that was facing problems very

much like the ones we grapple with today. We often imagine that the world Jesus came to was not complicated, that its problems were not complex. But historians tell us otherwise. They tell us that the problems of that day were similar to the problems of our day.

And right into the centre of this kind of life came Jesus Christ. He said, "Come unto me, all ye that labour and are heavy laden, and I will give you rest." And he said, "I am come that they might have life, and that they might have it more abundantly." Jesus had a healing word for everyone.

At this Christmas season, despite the affluent society that surrounds us, there are many who find life a burden. Purpose and zest have fled, hearts ache with emptiness, and even the joys of this happy season leave many of us lonely and wistful.

This Christmas the Lord Jesus Christ stands at the door of our hearts and knocks, saying, "If you will open that door, I will come in to you and sup with you, and you with me." Jesus wants to have Christmas with us.

Christmas means that "the Word was made flesh, and dwelt among us". Christmas means that Emmanuel has come – that "the people . . . in darkness have seen a great light" and that he walks with us through the shadows – it means that "God is with us". It means that our sordid, failure-fraught past can be wiped out by his sacrifice on the cross, and that we can become members of God's family, heirs of God and the citizens of heaven. Christmas means that he comes into the night of our suffering and sorrow, saying, "I am with you. Let me share your burdens."

During the Korean War one Christmas Eve a young marine lay dying on Heartbreak Ridge. The chaplain climbed up the slope and stooped over the marine and whispered, "May I help you, son?"

"No, it's all right", he answered.

The chaplain marvelled at the young man's complacency in such an hour; then, glancing down, the chaplain noticed a New Testament clutched in the marine's hand. And the reason for the young man's tranquillity was found on the page where his finger was inserted: "My peace I give unto you."

Today, in the midst of trouble, terrorism and war, that peace can be yours. It can come if you put your faith and trust in Jesus Christ. He is offering to every one of us eternal life if we will put our trust and our faith in him.

The gift of eternity can be ours now. "He who has the Son has life; he who has not the Son has not life." This is the real meaning of Christmas.

Will you accept Christ into your heart this Christmas season?

This Holy Night

God bless your house this holy night,
   And all within it;
God bless the candle that you light
   To midnight's minute:
The board at which you break your bread,
   The cup you drink of:
And as you raise it, the unsaid
   Name that you think of:
The warming fire, the bed of rest,
   The ringing laughter:
These things, and all things else be blest
   From floor to rafter
This holy night, from dark to light,
   Even more than other;
And, if you have no house tonight,
   God bless you, brother.

Eleanor Farjeon

✠

In the past, God spoke to our ancestors many times and in many ways through the prophets, but in these last days he has spoken to us through his Son. He is the one through whom God created the universe, the one whom God has chosen to possess all things at the end. He reflects the brightness of God's glory and is the exact likeness of God's own being, sustaining the universe with his powerful word. After achieving forgiveness for the sins of mankind, he sat down in heaven at the right-hand side of God, the Supreme Power.

(Hebrews 1:1–3)

In Case You Didn't Know . . .

Many of the contributors to this book have given their personal thoughts on the subject of Christmas. You might like to know more about them.

Eamonn Andrews
Eamonn Andrews has been the compere of many radio and television shows, but is known to millions as the presenter of Thames Television's "This Is Your Life". He also writes a weekly column for *The Universe*.

Marilyn Baker
Marilyn Baker was educated at a school for the blind before going on to study piano and oboe at the Royal School of Music. Her memorable songs, with their thought-provoking lyrics, have won her albums and performances a wide following.

The Revd Walter Barker
Walter Barker is Consultant to The Church's Ministry Among the Jews and has spent much time in Israel.

The Revd Richard Bewes
Richard Bewes is known to many for his pithy talks on BBC Radio's early-morning "Thought for the Day". He is Rector of All Souls, Langham Place, London – a stone's throw from the BBC's Broadcasting House.

Corrie ten Boom
Corrie ten Boom grew up in Holland and was imprisoned during World War II for protecting Jews. She later became an author and speaker who inspired many before her death in 1983.

The Revd Michael Bourdeaux
Michael Bourdeaux is General Director of Keston College, which specializes in the study of religious communities in the Soviet Union and Eastern Europe.

The Archbishop of Canterbury (The Most Revd and Rt Hon. Robert Runcie)
Formerly Bishop of St Albans, Dr Runcie became Archbishop of Canterbury in 1980.

Fiona Castle
Fiona Castle is particularly concerned for the role of the family in today's society, and is a regular contributor to the magazine *Christian Family*. She is married to entertainer Roy Castle.

Roy Castle
Roy Castle has been a well-known figure on stage and television for many years, recently on BBC TV's children's programme "Record Breakers".

Group Captain Leonard Cheshire VC, OM, DSO, DFC
Group Captain Cheshire served in Bomber Command from 1939 to 1945 and commanded the famous 617 Squadron – the Dambusters. He was the founder of the Leonard Cheshire Foundation Homes for the Disabled, which operate two hundred homes in forty-four countries. With his wife, Baroness Ryder, he was also co-founder of the Ryder Cheshire Mission for the Relief of Suffering.

James Fox
This well-known actor has given pleasure with his performances in numerous films, among them *The Servant, Those Magnificent Men in Their Flying Machines* and *A Passage to India*. He told his own story in *Comeback*.

Dr Billy Graham
Dr Graham is probably the world's best-known evangelist, who addresses vast crowds in every country he visits. He is also the author of many books.

Nicholas Hinton CBE
Nicholas Hinton is the Director General of The Save the Children Fund.

Bruce Kent
Bruce Kent was the General Secretary of the Campaign for Nuclear Disarmament from 1980 to 1985, and is frequently to be heard on television and radio. He has written many articles on nuclear disarmament, Christianity and peace.

The Countess of Swinton, Baroness Masham of Ilton
Baroness Masham was tragically injured in a horse-riding accident that left her substantially paralysed. She now endeavours to improve life for the disabled and was the founder of the Spinal Injuries Association, as well as serving on numerous committees.

John Motson
John Motson is a well-known football commentator, whose voice has been heard on BBC TV's "Match of the Day" since 1971. He has covered FA Cup, European Championship and World Cup finals and is the author of two books on football, as well as many newspaper and magazine articles.

Malcolm Muggeridge
Malcolm Muggeridge, now 84, was a journalist for many years and became a household name for his frequent appearances on television and radio and for his opinions on Christianity and related issues. He is the author of many books, including *Jesus Rediscovered* and *Something Beautiful for God*.

The Rt Hon. Lord Murray of Epping Forest OBE
Lord Murray became General Secretary of the Trades Union Congress in 1973 and retired in 1984.

Nick Page
Nick Page is a broadcaster with BBC Radio 2. He has presented many programmes, including "Sunday Half-Hour" and Radio 4's weekly service for primary schools.

Dr Luis Palau
Argentinian evangelist Luis Palau has spoken to millions of people all over the world through his crusades and television appearances. He is also the author of many books.

Ann Parkinson
Ann Parkinson is the wife of a leading politician and is deeply concerned with the problems and welfare of others.

The Bishop of Peterborough (The Rt Revd William Westwood)
Bishop Westwood became Bishop of Peterborough in 1984. He broadcasts frequently on BBC Radio and is a religious Adviser to the Independent Broadcasting Authority.

Gerald Priestland
Gerald Priestland was a BBC correspondent for thirty-three years, his posts ranging from "Today in Parliament" to Delhi, Beirut and Washington, and ultimately Religious Affairs. His talks, "Yours Faithfully" and "Priestland's Progress", were enormously popular and were made into successful books.

Cliff Richard
Cliff Richard's popularity never diminishes and it is incredible to recall that he began his singing career in the 1950s. He is the author of several books, including *Which One's Cliff?*

The Rt Hon. Norman St John-Stevas

Norman St John-Stevas has had a long political career, serving as MP for Chelmsford for many years and as leader of the House of Commons and Minister of Arts from 1979 to 1981. He retired as a Member of Parliament in 1987, and is now Chairman of the Royal Fine Art Commission.

Dame Cicely Saunders DBE

Dame Cicely Saunders is the founder of St Christopher's Hospice and indeed the whole hospice movement. In St Christopher's, gentle care allows those terminally ill to die with dignity.

Delia Smith

An inspired cook, Delia Smith communicates her skills both on television and in her immensely popular cookery books.

Adrian Snell

Adrian Snell is a composer, keyboard player and singer who communicates his Christian faith in the wider world of the arts. He has toured extensively and performed on radio and television all over the world. His best-known work, *The Passion*, was recorded with the Royal Philharmonic Orchestra.

The Revd the Lord Soper

At the age of 84, Lord Soper is still a frequent participant in television and radio discussions. A former President of the Methodist Conference, he still preaches each week from his Hyde Park soapbox.

Alvin Stardust

Alvin Stardust's singing career has spanned twenty-five years. In 1986 he co-presented BBC TV's "Rock Gospel Show" with Sheila Walsh. Very much a family man, he has also compiled several books, acted on stage, and is now working on a series for television.

John Timpson

For fifteen years John Timpson rose at 4 a.m. to present BBC Radio's "Today" programme to an audience of millions. He retired from "Today" in 1986 but continues to host Radio 4's "Any Questions".

The Rt Hon. Viscount Tonypandy

Viscount Tonypandy was Speaker of the House of Commons for many years. He has had a long and varied political career and written a number of books, including his memoirs.

The Revd Dr Chad Varah OBE

Dr Varah founded the Samaritans, of which he is now President. The Samaritans provide a 24–hour, confidential telephone support service for people facing crisis in their lives. Each year they listen to and befriend an increasing number of desperate, lonely and suicidal people.

Joanna Wade

Joanna Wade is a solicitor who first became involved with Crisis at Christmas as a student. She is now a committee member and has helped at eleven of the charity's "Open Christmases".

Sheila Walsh

Sheila Walsh's singing career took off when she was spotted performing in a church hall. She has since become one of the world's leading gospel singers, who is known for her best-selling albums and worldwide concerts, and as presenter of BBC TV's "Rock Gospel Show".

David Winter

David Winter is an author, broadcaster and Head of Religious Programmes for BBC Radio.

Acknowledgements

The Editor and publishers are grateful to the copyright holders for their permission to reprint the following material in this anthology:

Bible quotations, except where indicated, are from the Good News Bible, copyright © 1966, 1971 and 1976 American Bible Society, published by The Bible Societies/Collins.

Marilyn Baker, "God Came Among Us", copyright © Word Music (UK); reprinted by permission of Marilyn Baker and Word Music (UK).

John Betjeman, "Advent 1955", from *Uncollected Poems*, John Murray (Publishers) Ltd.

Rachel Billington, "A Christmas Story"; reprinted by permission of the author and *The Universe*.

Corrie ten Boom, "A Christmas Wish", from *Clippings From My Notebook*, Triangle/SPCK.

Eric Boswell, "Little Donkey", copyright © 1959 Chappell Music Ltd, London W1Y 3FA; reprinted by permission of Chappell Music Ltd and International Music Publications.

Fiona Castle, an article originally titled "I was torn between present-giving and helping"; reprinted by permission of *Christian Family* magazine.

Jean Chapman, "Robin's Red Breast", from *The Sugar Plum Christmas Book*, Hodder & Stoughton (Australia) Pty Ltd, 1977.

Leonard Clark, "Bells Ringing", from *Singing in the Streets: Poems for Christmas*, Dobson Books Ltd.

T.S. Eliot, an extract from *Murder in the Cathedral*, Faber & Faber Ltd.

Eleanor Farjeon, "Keeping Christmas", "The Ending of the Year" and "This Holy Night", from *Silver Sand and Snow*, Michael Joseph Ltd; reprinted by permission of David Higham Associates Ltd.

Delia Smith, an extract from *A Feast for Advent*, Bible Reading Fellowship.

Adrian Snell & Phil Thomson, "How Can I Explain?", from *The Virgin*, recorded by Pilgrim Records and published by Coronation Music; reprinted by permission of Adrian Snell and Marshall Pickering.

Dylan Thomas, an extract from *A Child's Christmas in Wales*, J.M. Dent & Sons Ltd; reprinted by permission of David Higham Associates Ltd.

John Timpson, "That Early Morning in Bethlehem", from *John Timpson's Early Morning Book*, Collins Publishers.

Steve Turner, "Christmas Is Really For The Children", from *Up to Date*, copyright © 1976, 1980, 1982 by Steve Turner; reprinted by permission of Hodder & Stoughton Ltd.

David Winter, an extract from *Truth in the Son*, copyright © 1985 by David Winter; reprinted by permission of Hodder & Stoughton Ltd.

Richard Wurmbrand, an extract from *In God's Underground*, W.H. Allen Publishers.

Special thanks to the staff and pupils of St Joseph's Roman Catholic First and Middle School, Harrow, and Stag Lane First School, Edgware, for the children's quotes.

Every effort has been made to contact the copyright holders, but in a few cases this has proved impossible. We apologize for any omission, which will be corrected in any future edition.

Crisis at Christmas

The royalties from the sale of this book are going to help Crisis at Christmas, a registered charity with no particular religious or political bias which has been working in the field of homelessness since 1967.

The charity's aim is to alleviate the suffering of those who are homeless and alone. To this end it raises money for distribution to projects throughout the UK. Crisis is also involved in educational work and in running its famous annual Open Christmas for the homeless in London.

If you would like to find out more about Crisis at Christmas or make a contribution to their work, please write to:

Crisis at Christmas,
212 Whitechapel Road,
London E1 1BJ.